A Step-By-Step Guide To Recovery For All Adult Survivors And Co-dependents

Mohan S. Nair, M.D.

Health Communications, Inc.
Deerfield Beach, Florida

Library of Congress Cataloging-in-Publication Data

Nair, Mohan, 1950
   A step-by-step guide to recovery for all adult survivors and co-
   dependents / Mohan Nair.
      p.   cm.
   ISBN 1-55874-114-3
   1. Adult children of dysfunctional families.   2. Co-dependence
   (Psychology)   I. Title.
RC455.4.F3N35   1990   90-4892
616.86—dc20   CIP

Publisher: Health Communications, Inc.
              3201 S.W. 15th Street
              Deerfield Beach, Florida 33442-8190

ACKNOWLEDGMENTS

Enduring thanks to Harold Davidson, M.D., my guide and proctor at Harvard, for his wisdom, kindness and patience.

To Virginia, for providing me the "space" to write this book, by her countless efforts.

To my teachers, whose excitement kindled my own excitement about the mind and the brain.

To Jenny Francis and David Victorson, my friends in the recovery community, who took me beyond the scientific.

To my wife, Brady, for her unconditional love.

And to my children: Maya, Amar and Raj, for being there and making everything so wonderful.

DEDICATION

This book is dedicated to my parents, whose unselfish love made all things possible.

FOREWORD

A Step-By-Step Guide To Recovery For All Adult Survivors and Co-dependents is an important work that makes a powerful statement to professionals and lay people alike. Dr. Mohan Nair beautifully illustrates the connection between co-dependency and child abuse. Further, he offers treatment strategies that are dynamic, useful and clinically sound. With a background in psychiatry and years of experience in treating co-dependents, Dr. Nair incorporates his medical framework with a 12-Step tradition — an unusual and potent combination. *A Step-By-Step Guide To Recovery For All Adult Survivors and Co-dependents* effectively confronts the travesty of misdiagnosis and over-medication of child abuse survivors in a way that is insightful and direct.

All in all, Dr. Nair deals with a very delicate and pervasive issue in a way that will no doubt bring relief and healing to thousands of child abuse survivors.

Rokelle Lerner

CONTENTS

INTRODUCTION

What is hell?
Hell is oneself,
The other figures in it, merely projections.

T. S. Elliot

I don't believe that people were meant to be unhappy and I don't think that most people want to be unhappy. It is my belief that most people who suffer from chronic unhappiness, from serious emotional and behavioral disturbances such as addictions and co-dependency are caught in the nightmare of their childhood and are struggling to work their way out. Sometimes they lack awareness.

This is a book about total recovery for people, such as incest survivors and children of alcoholics, who have grown up in a dysfunctional, abusive early childhood environment. It will help take them from the miseries of enslavement — to others as in co-dependency, and enslavement to alcohol, chemicals, food, sex and the various psychiatric and medical labels — on to empowerment, self-love and self-confidence.

In a step-by-step manner it tells you how to recognize the effects of growing up in a dysfunctional family and how to overcome them without drugs and endless therapy. It shows you how to use your own inner spiritual strength, along with the 12 Steps and positive and humane tools, such as massage, exercise, self-soothing skills and self-awareness techniques, to work towards total recovery.

This book was written for co-dependents, addicts and those who carry the various labels of mental illness, such as major depression, manic-depressive illness, panic anxiety disorders, obsessive-compulsive-impulsive disorders, psychotic disorders, sexual dysfunction and borderline personality disorders. And it is also for those who, in spite of knowing that they are courageous, intelligent and caring, seem to find it difficult to live with themselves and others and are torn by feelings of self-doubt, self-hate, loneliness and powerlessness.

It is about loving, about learning how to love oneself.

This book grew out of my 12 years of experience in working with abuse survivors, young and old. It came out of the awareness and the recognition that all of us have within ourselves, the seeds of joy and meaning in our lives.

Out
Of The
Darkness

ONE

Defining The Darkness

The heresy of one age becomes the orthodoxy of the next.

Helen Keller

Darkness is the lack of awareness — self-awareness and awareness of things around you. To fight your way out of it, you need knowledge — knowledge of what you have been fighting and what you need to win the fight.

All co-dependent and addictive behaviors, most "psychiatric" and many physical illnesses have their roots, this book firmly maintains, in a dysfunctional family environment. Other common factors among addicts and co-dependents are:

- Lack of self-awareness.
- Lack of self-soothing.

3

- Lack of self-esteem.
- Lack of self-empowerment.

These deficiencies are present by the time a child is three years old. From then on they can decrease or be made worse.

By corollary, a child who has had a "good-enough mothering," a good-enough parenting until the age of three, is relatively invulnerable to co-dependency, addictive behaviors and most psychiatric illnesses. People who grow up in an environment of love and respect don't abuse themselves, sell themselves short or abuse others.

Because the wounds of shame, rage, hopelessness and lack of nurturing are at a *nonverbal,* preverbal level, they are contained in the unconscious and in the body. Following are some of the "givens" I've identified as part of the process of true recovery from these deeply buried hurts.

1. No amount of "talk therapy" alone will help recovery and it often can be harmful and enabling. Medications are rarely helpful and are often dangerous to people in recovery.
2. Massage, body work and exercise are necessary to heal the wounds of childhood, to trigger memories and to find real power and a sense of oneself. Without these elements, many, if not most people will not be in recovery.
3. Also, no recovery from co-dependency and addictive illness or other problems arising out of having grown up in a dysfunctional family environment is possible without the rigorous working of the 12 Steps.
4. Spiritual recovery is an essential part in the recovery by the 12-Step method.
5. Remembering childhood and its associated trauma as completely as possible is part of inventory taking and absolutely essential towards recovery and growth.
6. A 12-Step recovery program that involves body work, massage, exercise and memory work should allow a person with co-dependency, addiction problems and many psychologic and behavioral problems to be free of the need of ongoing psychotherapy and medications within six months to a year.
7. All help is directed toward the encouragement of self-help.

Co-dependency

Co-dependency is a condition in which one person's thoughts, feelings and behaviors are influenced to such a degree by another person's (or persons') thoughts, feelings and behaviors that it causes emotional/physical pain or illness and/or takes away from the person's capacity to grow, blossom, be creative or find meaning and joy in life. At one end of the spectrum is the overtly physically-abused wife with an alcoholic or a drug addict husband. Often she is financially supporting the alcoholic-addict. At the other end of the spectrum is the great number of bright and wonderful women (and men) who have given up their own dreams to be caught up in the dreams of a "significant other," usually a parent or a spouse, sometimes a friend, employer or organization: the society wife who sells herself short, stifling her creativity to glow only in her husband's or boyfriend's glory; the nurse who puts her life on hold to send her husband through medical school, only to be dumped in the end, feeling great bitterness; the many who are drawn into powerful friendships which call for the relentless "giving" of money, effort and creativity, then find themselves cheated and empty-handed. Also, people drawn into cults or criminal organizations are among them. The list is endless.

Addictions

Addictions are a condition in which a person becomes emotionally (and often physically) dependent on a substance, action or a lifestyle to such a degree that being deprived of the substance, action or lifestyle will cause emotional and/or physical distress. The craving has a compulsive overpowering quality and there is a tendency towards increasing use and participation. Examples of drugs, alcohol, food and sexually deviant behavior such as sadomasochism, cross-dressing and pedophilia.

Abuse

Abuse takes place when a person in power does not respect the physical and emotional boundaries of another person. The power may be emotional, physical or financial. It can be the overt physical and sexual abuse of a minor by parents and parentlike figures or extended family members.

More subtle abuses take place when children are not allowed to dream for themselves and an adult's dreams, desires, needs or urges are forced upon them. Conditional love, too, can often be emotionally abusive.

Second-Stage Recovery

Second-stage recovery is the process, after giving up the addiction, of dealing with the flood of unresolved feelings and memories of childhood and adolescence, and of growing up in a dysfunctional environment. Not working through the second stage causes relapse or another addiction.

TWO

Surrender

*He who would be cured of ignorance must con-
fess to it.*

Montaigne

Admitting to the problem is a difficult first step because you may not know that something is not right with your life. People who grow up in families that are alcoholic, incestuous, physically abusive or otherwise shaming or discounting don't know what it is like to be treated with respect and noncontingent love — being loved for themselves. All they know about is being abused and disrespected and being "something for someone else." This is especially true for women. Adult children of alcoholics and abuse survivors are abusive to themselves and others, sell themselves short, hold back their potential and may live a lifetime through two and three generations of family and never define the problem.

Recognizing Denial, Repression And Dissociation

Denial, repression and dissociation are important defenses that may have helped you live through the days and nights of growing up in a dysfunctional environment — a continuing nightmare. However, now it cripples you. But keep in mind, most of all, that if you are living a life that is joyless, abusive to yourself and others, you need to take a second look. Ignorance is not bliss. Remember, the children of God were not meant to be the slaves of man.

It is an important first step in self-awareness to identify the nature of your suffering. The memories and feelings of an abusive childhood cannot be tied into a neat little bundle and cast away. It is like a poison that pervades your entire body and soul, your entire life. It is like nuclear waste, working its way into the very marrow of your existence, destroying your soul and poisoning those around you by its radiation. It tears you up on the inside and the outside, even when you don't see it and even when you don't know it. It takes away from your energy, your creativity, your physical health, the capacity to hug and be hugged, to make love, to work and to be creative. It takes away from your being a good parent, spouse, lover, friend, employee and employer. It disturbs your sleep with nightmares and it can wrack your body with migraine, colitis, stomach problems and a thousand other pains. It compulsively drives you to hurt yourself and others close to you.

It makes you scared and angry when people get close to you and it makes you scared, sad and angry when people move away from you. You are out of control, while all your energy goes towards making believe that you are in control.

The seeds of an abusive, discounting, shame- and rage-filled childhood grow into a tree with many branches. Take the time to identify the branches. It is a good place to start.

The results of abuse in your childhood affect your body and mind, your mood, your behavior, your thoughts and your relationships. These changes from the normal could be seen ever since childhood. You need to take a good look but, remember, surrendering is not easy. There will be many temptations to put back that armor. There will be many times when you will rush back to your well-known defenses of denial, repression and dissociation. Making change is frightening. However, be clear that running away is not making change.

THREE

Second-Stage Recovery: Knowing And Remembering

Start out, in the process of second stage recovery, with the thought that maybe your childhood was not as rosy as you recall it to be — or was even more horrible.

Every human being gets hurt in the process of growing up. That is part of life. For many of us, these wounds are small and the family environment that we grew up in healed them to various degrees. It is a sense of being wounded and not being able to turn to those who are supposed to love and protect that leaves one with a sense of betrayal and feelings of abandonment. The results of feeling abandonment are rage, hopelessness and boredom. Rage against parents causes guilt. This guilt is turned into self-hate.

Rage, Boredom And Hopelessness

It is the rage and hopelessness that has not been dealt with that hurts and takes away from the capacity for self love and joy. It makes people sick emotionally and physically over a period of time, especially when the very reasons for this hate have been suppressed.

11

Hopelessness is not an adult feeling. Boredom is not an adult feeling. Rage is not an adult feeling. Rage, boredom and hopelessness are remnants of unresolved feelings of childhood when there was truly nowhere to turn, when poeple who were supposed to love and protect you turned against you and then you turned around and made believe that this didn't happen. It was better to believe that your parents were good, even if it meant that you were the bad one.

Rage

Rage is a feeling of childhood and infancy, especially chronic rage. Unlike anger, rage is not a feeling that has a name or a face. It consumes a person. The roots of chronic and explosive rage come from a preverbal time, from infancy, from a child that felt abandoned or unloved. Anytime I see a person who is chronically in rage, I know that she or he has been the child of an unhappy, apathetic mother who herself felt unrespected and unloved, often a mother who is in a co-dependent relationship with an alcoholic or an addict of some kind, who is incapable of giving love — noncontingent love, love without strings attached. Often such a mother comes from a home where she has seen her own mother being abused and disrespected by her father. She herself usually, if not always, has been abused and discounted and not allowed to feel proud of being a woman. She feels vulnerable and ashamed about her womanhood. She has always looked outside for validating herself. This is the background of a budding rageaholic. Many addicts, when they give up drugs and alcohol, become the rageaholics that they had been suppressing with the alcohol or the drugs.

Another reason for chronic rage comes from having been at the receiving end of rage as an infant. Said David, a patient of mine: "I grew up scared — scared of my father beating me up and beating up my mother and my sisters. They were little and I wanted to protect them. I wanted to kill him. I'm 27 now and I'm in therapy and attending ACoA [Adult Children Of Alcoholics] because of physically hurting my three-year-old son when he was a year old. He was screaming and a rage overtook me and I could hear the scream of my father's voice in my head like an explosion: 'Shut up, you little fucker.' And I hit him, my little baby boy who's the best thing in my life — my little baby boy who had just begun to walk. I have always had tremendous rage and stayed in the military because it seemed like a good place to lose control, to get into fights and still be accepted, still be a man."

It is an important part of recovery to learn, first of all, to acknowledge hidden rage and then, as one begins to recall where the rage came from, names, faces and events coming to mind will allow the sufferer of rage to work through them, converting the rage into *anger* toward specific people and events.[1] Anger is mature, appropriate and less consuming, less overwhelming and is less likely to hurt the body.[2]

In my experience, most men from ACA backgrounds who have witnessed their mothers being beaten have felt homicidal towards their fathers or stepfathers. It is a terrible thought for a child to carry in his head. Remember, "Honor thy father and thy mother." This guilt often makes him suicidal. So he hovers between suicide and homicide. The reason why he feels homicidal is because he feels castrated. For a male child deeply enmeshed with his mother, his inability to protect her causes him to feel less than a man at a time when being and becoming a man is everything. One way in which he deals with such murderous feelings is to dissociate from such feelings and identify with the aggressor, continuing the process of becoming a wife beater and child abuser himself.

Untreated rage leads to episodic and persistent violence by adolescents and to efforts to control the rage by the use of alcohol. By this time, alcohol feels like a welcome relief from such agony. As a person gets older — in their 30s, 40s and 50s — the violence may decrease but physical illnesses brought on by feeling rage all the time continue to worsen. Letting go of alcohol often brings back the feelings that were suppressed in the first place. This is what second stage recovery is about.

Hopelessness

All adult children of dysfunctional families have feelings of hopelessness — either chronic or coming and going, seemingly with no reason. Like rage, hopelessness speaks of a failure of parental love, of abandonment, shaming and very often overt abuse and dehumanizing experiences, including sexual abuse. It suggests a background of having a co-dependent depressed mother, sunk in apathy and self-pity, unable to be excited by or enjoy her infant. Chronic or episodic intense hopelessness is due to a childhood and an infancy where truly there was nowhere to turn.

Adults always have choices. Children have to deal with hopelessness on a daily basis, waking up to it and going to bed with it. Such intense hopelessness can actually destroy the body of the child.

Dissociation, denial and repression become ways of dealing with such feelings, allowing the child to live through the agony — until they find addictions: religion, drugs, alcohol and/or work. Addictions reinforce denial.

Hopelessness calls for a journey into childhood, to reach out, be available to and communicate with your inner child.

Boredom

Boredom is the half-brother of hopelessness, a feeling midway between rage and hopelessness. It is the quality of people who are not *self-sufficient.* Not self-sufficient because of not being given noncontingent love, affection and excitement. It suggests an infancy with a mother who is unexcited about her child, apathetic and nervous, without the capacity to self-soothe. Only a mother who can soothe herself can truly soothe her child. The child withdraws into a void, an emptiness of the soul, so that it doesn't have to feel.

Boredom is a destructive feeling. It causes the person to feel lonely even in the midst of people. Risk-taking, thrill-seeking behaviors, hedonistic pursuits are efforts to deal with boredom. So are addictions. Drugs like alcohol and heroin can draw you into a womblike comfort. Speed and cocaine can bring temporary excitement. Self-mutilation can let you know that you are alive.

Excessive and premature interest in sex takes place, evidenced by masturbating and putting things inside the vagina and/or rectum. Later this again surfaces as perversions and sexual addictions, even in the absence of overt sexual abuse. It can be at once soothing and exciting for the child who knows no soothing or excitement. It is an effort not to feel dead.

Boredom. Hopelessness. Rage. These are terrible and painful feelings that will hit addicts and co-dependents weeks and months into recovery. You cannot run away from it because they are coming from within you. It can often throw you into a relapse. Acknowledging, remembering, feeling and working through the memories of grief and rage is what second stage recovery is all about.

Psychiatric/Medical Symptoms In Survivors

The psychiatric problems of adult survivors of abuse, of co-dependents and addicts are often either discredited, minimized or terribly misdiagnosed as illnesses such as schizophrenia, manic-depressive illness, major depressive disorder, sexual perversions, eating disorders or anxiety panic disorders. They are often mistreated after diagnosis with shock therapy and mind-numbing, mind-damaging and addictive medications. Sometimes they are diagnosed purely as physical illnesses without the underlying psychologic reasons ever being touched.

Early childhood abuse should be suspected in all the conditions listed below:

Chronic gastrointestinal problems.
Anorexia nervosa.
Chronic fatigue syndrome.
Anxiety panic with hyperventilation, palpitations of the heart and numbness of the arms and feet.
Severe premenstrual syndrome.

The awareness of having grown up in an alcoholic family should further compound such a suspicion.

Amnesia For Childhood Events

Amnesia regarding the early years is particularly severe with people who have been abused as children, especially sexually abused. Sometimes a teenager or a child is confronted with the choice of taking a physical beating inflicted by an abusive parent or learning to "cooperate" sexually. How does a little girl go from playing "child whore" to satisfy her step-parent at night, play mother in the evenings and go to school and be a seven-year-old first grader? She does this by *dissociation.* Dissociation is the mechanism involved in dealing with very severe abuse. The earliest and the most painful wounds of childhood are handled by this method. Anytime there are large gaps in the memory of childhood, one needs to suspect the possibility of abuse, especially sexual abuse, possibly even ritual abuse. The possibility of ritual abuse should be suspected even more strongly if the person compulsively engages in self-mutilation, especially mutilation of the genital area.

---

1. Maternal depression and apathy during infancy (common in co-dependents), abandonment and physical abuse by father, mother, siblings; torture.

2. Rage is believed to be at the roots of hypertension, colitis, migraine headaches and ulcers. Anger can be worked through at a cognitive (an understanding and thinking) level.

FOUR

Looking For
Signs Of Abuse

From infancy through childhood, through adolescence, into adulthood and continuing in old age, people who have been abused feel, act and think differently from those who have not been abused. These differences are important to look for in people you love, (including yourself) if you suspect the possibility of abuse in their background, if they are unaware of it and if you feel they would be receptive to your observations.

Following is a summary of the behavioral, medical and interpersonal characteristics common to the four stages of life.

1. In Infancy

The abused infant behaves in an apathetic or restless manner. He or she has a greater tendency towards constant rocking. Either there is excessive crying or there is a tremendous lack of crying in an abnormal manner, clearly suggesting a situation in which there is no response to normal crying. The infant also shows an exaggerated startle response.

Medical Problems Of Abused Infants

Medical problems of abused infants include failure to thrive, sleep disturbances, gastrointestinal disturbances, injuries caused by abusers or by masturbation to genital area and infections of the genital area. The child looks very limp (hypotonia). Its mood is apathetic or irritable and the child connects to what is happening and to people very poorly. In interacting with people, the child may be very clingy, may not show appropriate response to strangers or may be very distant.

2. In Childhood

During this time, children of abuse may be diagnosed as having the following problems:

- Reactive attachment disorder.
- Mental retardation.
- Tourette's.
- Gender identity problems.
- Mutism.

A whole host of medical and neurologic problems may be described. They may complain of headaches, gastrointestinal problems and constipation (a constant state of tension making it difficult for the child to evacuate its bowels). Think of how difficult it is to go to the bathroom in great fear. The child may show urinary tract problems and genital area injuries if it is being sexually abused. Injuries should also be suspected in males as a result of sexual abuse (anal rectal injury).

Both in infants and children, broken bones and concussions need to be looked into carefully for the possibility of abuse. The child growing up within an abusive home is depressed, anxious, angry, jealous, apathetic, sometimes extremely manic and often excessively timid. Its thoughts and perceptions are chronically preoccupied with low self-esteem and self-hate.

The child may have auditory or visual hallucinations and paranoia, and is often delusional. On inquiring, the child may describe wanting to be dead or wanting to kill someone. It may have obsessive-compulsive behaviors such as excessive hand washing and may show ritual behavior such as an excessive need to have everything in order. This preoccupation with order and arranging things in an orderly manner within their room or around them may often be diagnosed as obsessive-compulsive behavior or autism. The child might become a bully with peers and schoolmates. It may be abused by other children within its group and may often become a scapegoat. Or the child may have no peer group at all. Memory problems are often seen.

The Abused Child's Interpersonal Relationships

Abused children are often abusive and clingy, often with inappropriate touching. At other times they react violently to touch. Their interactions with adults are often idolizing or devaluing with rapid shifts from one to the other, behaviors often continuing as they become teenagers and adults.

If seen by psychiatrists and psychologists, they are often diagnosed by their symptoms with the root cause never being found out. These include:

Depression.
Hyperactivity with attention deficit disorder.
Learning disabilities.
"Pervasive developmental disorder."
Tourette's.
Functional encopresis.
Functional enuresis.
Autism.
Conduct disorder of an oppositional type.
Separation anxiety disorder.
Over-anxious disorder.

3. The Adolescent Abuse Survivor

The adolescent abuse survivor behaves in a hyperactive or withdrawn manner. They may be excessively timid, aggressive or sexualized. Compulsive masturbation, sexual acting out, promiscuous behavior, molesting other children, running away, truancy and school failure are common.

However, teenagers from dysfunctional homes may go a different route and become overachievers so that they don't have to deal with the nightmare of their home lives. Unpredictable, suicidal, self-destructive behavior and, of course, increasing involvement with drugs and alcohol, should cause strong concern about the possibility of abuse. Self-mutilation, involvement with Satan worship, gender iden-

tity problems and sudden changes in sexual preference and homosexual acting out should cause concern as to the cause.

Medical Problems Of Teenagers Who Have Been Abused

Headaches.
Chest pain and palpitations.
Insomnia, sleep-walking and nightmares.
Loss of bladder and bowel control.
Gastrointestinal problems.
Genitourinary problems including menstrual irregularities and
    pelvic cysts.
Genital and/or rectal injuries.
Disturbances of sleep, appetite and energy levels (constant fatigue
    or agitation).
Impaired attention and concentration.

Moods

Moods vary between depression and rage, fear, anxiety and boredom. There are sharp shifts in mood from rage to hopelessness
without apparent reasons.

Thought problems include perceptions of grandiosity, paranoid
feelings, low self-esteem and self-hate. They may show extreme
forgetfulness and delusions (false beliefs), pressured thinking and
fragmentation of their thoughts (becoming very scattered in their
thinking and reasoning). This may cause them to be diagnosed as
psychotic by psychiatrists and to be put on medications.

Interpersonal Behavior

Dealing with other peers and adults often becomes unstable. The
teenager may become very isolative, distant or aggressive. By this
time, masochistic, sadistic, sexualized and people-pleasing behavior
may all be seen. A tremendous urge to belong will often gravitate
a teenager at this point towards other angry and often abused peers
who become involved with crime, drugs, gangs, Satanism and prostitution or who drop out of school or ran away.

If seen by psychologists and psychiatrists at this time, they may
be diagnosed as depressed, manic-depressive and antisocial or as
having a conduct disorder.

4. In Adulthood

Survivors show the following conditions or behaviors:

Manic/hyperactive.

Isolative.

Chemically dependent.

Alcoholic.

Workaholic.

Underachiever.

Overachiever.

Sexualized.

Aggressive.

Suicidal.

Self-mutilative.

Deviant sexual behavior (molesting younger children, sex involving inflicting pain or pain having been inflicted on them, fetishism, pornography).

Extreme impulsivity.

Severe passivity.

Disturbance of sleep (too much, too little and always fatigued).

Disturbance of appetite (too much or too little).

Disturbance of energy levels (either having too much and uncontrolled energy or having no energy).

Legal problems related to violent, criminal behavior and substance abuse.

Adult sexual abuse survivors will often show both deviant sexual behavior such as exhibitionism, molesting young children and unrestrained and impulsive sexual activity. Males may be seen as sexual addicts. Extramarital affairs and multiple affairs in marriages are common. Girls will often become promiscuous or be exploited in sexual relationships, or engage in prostitution. Wife-beating and child abuse may be seen on the part of male abuse survivors. Women may become abusive towards their children. Both men and women may abandon their children. While this is more common with men, it appears to produce less guilt and depression but in women who abandon their children, self-destructive behaviors, lifestyles and chronic depression and its consequences are common.

Medical Problems Of Adult Survivors

These include headaches, dizzy spells and intense fatigue sometimes diagnosed as chronic fatigue syndrome.

Symptoms related to the chest and neck involve swallowing difficulties, choking sensations, chest pain and palpitations. Hyperventilation often causes feelings of numbness in the arms, legs and a burning sensation around the face. Mitral valve prolapse is often described by women.[1]

Gastrointestinal problems include peptic ulcer disease and irritable bowel syndrome, constipation and nervous diarrhea. Survivors who suffer from eating disorder and bulimia, nausea and forced vomiting may often have tears and scarring of their esophagus, often causing them great difficulty and pain while swallowing after they have had these symptoms for a long time.

Males with a history of alcoholism often have severe tears in the lower end of the esophagus where it joins the stomach, causing vomiting of blood.

Female organ problems are common among survivors. These include severe premenstrual syndrome, excessive bleeding, painful bleeding and swelling of the breasts and weight gain during the premenstrual period. Pelvic cysts and endometriosis are very common.[2]

Endocrine problems, including menstrual irregularities and thyroid abnormalities, including hypothyroidism and hyperthyroidism, are seen. *Sexually transmitted diseases* such as AIDS and herpes are common in abuse survivors, especially because of their choice of partners which is indiscriminate, impulsive and often multiple. The partners themselves are similar in nature, thereby doubly increasing the risks of veneral disease.

Mood Problems

Mood problems include chronic depression with periods of intense hopelessness that seem to occur for no particular reason. They may also be chronically anxious with phobias and panic attacks. Chronic angry feelings triggered off by minor changes in life and interactions with people are common. There are outbursts of rage, once again precipitated without any clear-cut reasons. These may often make the person violent towards themselves or others.

Disturbances In The Way Of Thinking

Disturbed thinking includes pressured and racing thoughts, circular thinking, extreme preoccupation and not being able to let go, false beliefs, a tendency to quickly believe, in a cultlike manner, without reflection, what a significant other believes; obsessive-compulsive thinking which may include continuously obsessing over injury or death of someone close by; house burning down, doors not being locked and the need to take showers frequently to the point of causing injury to the skin or hands by handwashing. Hallucinations and delusions may be present, *but need to be differentiated from hallucinations suffered by schizophrenics, whom adult survivors of child abuse are often mistaken for.* These hallucinations frequently become more intense and they come and go with seemingly normal periods between them. They are often precipitated by contact with people who trigger abuse-related feelings or occur when the person is alone. Hallucinations may include seeing things that are not there, such as the presence of a person standing close to them, especially when they are lying in bed. Auditory hallucinations include voices of little children within the person, screams and shouts of children and screaming sounds and shouting of adults in a fearful manner, suggestive of screaming and yelling heard by the adult survivor of a dysfunctional family when growing up.

Relationships Of Adult Survivors

The most significant symptom among adult survivors in relationships is that they do not perceive themselves as equal. They can either see themselves as being below someone or above someone. The relationships are often unstable and numerous, i.e., they come to know someone very quickly, fall in love with them and become intensely attached with great expectations, then become easily disappointed and rageful within the relationship. In essence, they are idolizing and devaluing. The same person who is abused in one relationship can often become the abuser in another relationship.

These patterns of relationship often cause the abuse survivor to be diagnosed as having a borderline personality disorder.

Abuse survivors may seek safety in abandoning relationships altogether and live in tremendous isolation. There are large numbers of people who avoid relationships altogether, especially sexual relationships, because they are so threatened.

Late- Middle- And Old-Age Behaviors

Co-dependents, abuse survivors and addicts continue to show a worsening of their adult behavior through maturity. Instead of life becoming increasingly more stable and connected, they become more isolative, workaholic and suicidal. Those who have problems with street drugs will often turn towards food, alcohol and prescription medications to replace heroin, cocaine and street-obtained downers. The capacity to play, relax and socialize in a meaningful manner continues to worsen. Old age is full of bitterness and loneliness with depressed and suicidal feelings and tremendous rage. The combination of alcoholism with the end results of severe liver disease, portal hypertension, heart disease and hypertension causes both metabolic as well as vascular injury in the brain, resulting in mental problems due to actual brain damage. This can lead to a person's becoming demented, paranoid, confused and delirious in their late 40s, 50s or 60s when people who come from a healthier background may be leading full and active lives with clear minds.

Medical Problems Of Older Survivors

By now, the abuse and neglect of the body, mind and the self has begun to cause the physical machinery to fail. Diseases brought about by poor eating habits, lack of exercise and internal stress begin to wear it down continuously. Cardiovascular disease such as strokes and paralysis are common. Impotence because of the physiologic complications of hypertension, peripheral vascular disease and diabetes are seen at an early age. Cancers of the mouth, tongue and lungs caused by smoking, and bowel cancer are commonly seen. Chronic back pain is worsened by obesity and lack of exercise. Early death, crippling disabilities caused by neglect of the body, and intense sense of isolation and abandonment by family members are experienced.

Feelings Of Older Co-dependents And Addicts

Depression, apathy, periods of unexplained anger and rage and mood swings are common among older co-dependents. Anxiety symptoms, panic attacks and phobias are frequently seen with the female population. The thinking of adult co-dependents and other untreated abuse survivors continues to focus on low self-esteem, an inability to do any creative thinking, increasing loss of memory and confusion because of medical problems described previously. Paranoia is intensified by chronic alcoholism-related brain damage. Because of a lack of support system, they often become wards of state-run facilities where they continue to be abused by others within the system.

1. Mitral valve prolapse is a common condition found approximately in one out of seven women, with excessive tissue in the mitral valve and elongated chordae tendineae (the cables that connect the valves to the muscle of the heart). Most patients remain asymptomatic. Common symptoms include chest pain, supraventricular and ventricular arrhythmias. Complications are severe mitral regurgitation resulting in left ventricular failure. Rarely, emboli are deposited on the valve. Sudden death is a very rare complication. The symptoms of mitral valve prolapse appear to be common in people, especially women, who are prone to severe anxiety. Medication commonly prescribed is Inderal. Echocardiograms are helpful in determining the mitral valve abnormality but as indicated earlier, the abnormality itself may not cause symptoms.

2. Anytime I see a patient with multiple pelvic surgeries or an early hysterectomy, I am suspicious of sexual abuse. Forty percent of women who have had multiple laparoscopies (where a gynecologist puts a scope through a little hole in the stomach and looks inside) have been sexually abused in childhood.

FIVE

Remembering Childhood

It takes two to tell the truth — one to speak it and the other to hear.

Thoreau

The task of recovery is not an easy one and can only happen if you are desperate about it. It must become the most important thing in your life.

There is a little child inside you that, in loneliness and in secret, knows, feels and remembers. Reach out to your inner child.

You have to begin to give up the armor that has saved you from having to feel all those terrible feelings of childhood. This armor includes denial, repression, dissociation ("spacing out") and amnesia (loss of memory for childhood events).

For those who have acquired chemical addictions, the armor is even harder to peel away. When you were young you reached out for the alcohol and the drugs and felt grateful that they made you numb — numbed the thoughts that you didn't want to think and the feelings that you didn't want to feel. It may be months, sometimes years, after a person becomes sober until they will be able to start thinking and feeling and asking questions about their childhood. This is the beginning of second stage recovery.

This stage may start only if they have not gone into another addiction or escaped into another abusive or hedonistic relationship or some other avenue (including slavish and co-dependent work habits) of finding false self-esteem.

Knowing will free you. There was a time when no one asked and no one cared or you were punished for speaking out. Don't become the abusing adult and repeat the mistakes of your parents by discounting these feelings. Get on your knees and put your ear close to that little voice in your heart. You cannot hear the voice, the moans, the whimpers and the screams if you have someone screaming at you (husband, boyfriend, boss or friend) or you have to take care of someone else before you can take care of yourself.

You cannot listen to your inner child in a bar. Alcoholics Anonymous (AA) is a good place to start. However, if you come from an alcoholic background, you need to attend ACA 12-Step meetings as well. You need to acquire a sponsor from the ACA meetings. If you are an incest survivor, you need to attend 12-Step incest survivor meetings. There with people of a common wounding, without shame, you can begin to speak and you can begin to listen — listen to things that will make you tremble, make you nauseous, make you feel like you want to scream, cause you to have flashbacks and wild mood swings and tear up your sleep with nightmares. The danger of going back to drugs, alcohol and abusive relationships will come to you again and again like a safe haven. Don't take that route. *Recovery is difficult but possible. No one can do it other than yourself.*

Again, you have to start asking questions about your childhood. It may help you to talk to parents for some of the answers. Be prepared for vague answers, guilt trips ("We did the best we could" or "I didn't leave him because I didn't want to break up the family and leave you without a father"), outright denial ("It is not like what you think" or "That's not true").

An example of confrontation with the past is given by a woman I'll call Zelda. Four months into treatment Zelda had a frightening flashback that left her weak and tearful. The scene took place when she was five years old, after she made a comment about her father's deformed right leg. He took her aside and hammered a nail through her knee, then drove her to an emergency room and told the doctor that she had fallen on a nail. She confronted her father with this. He denied it completely. He told her that she was crazy. However, the patient stayed with her memories and in time began to uncover more memories of incestuous sexual abuse. This abuse had left her with a lifetime of self-doubt, self-hate, sexually destructive behaviors, abusive relationships and an inability to maintain any kind of stable lifestyle. She had made multiple suicide attempts and struggled with eating disorders and chemical dependency.

Talk to your siblings. Talk to family members who are positive figures in your early childhood. Look into your photo albums. Look through your scrapbooks. Look through your yearbook. Pay attention to your flashbacks and your dreams. Drive around your old neighborhood.

Seeking Support As You Search

A warning: this questioning will make you feel more than uncomfortable. You will feel depressed, rageful, shameful, murderous and maybe even suicidal. It may cause you to feel sexually excited with an even increasing sense of guilt and self-hate. It may make you feel shaky and weak like you are going to pass out. It will make you feel dirty. It may make you feel scared.

Have a close friend or a spouse or your therapist hold your hand or soothe you if you can do it without worrying about *them.* If you are alone, soothe your neck, head, arms, legs and shoulders by stroking and massaging to keep you centered and prevent you from dissociating. Take frequent showers if you feel "dirty." Exercise when you feel weak. Use a punching bag when you need to. Take breaks when you have to but *always* get back as soon as you are able to. Above all, never lose sight of the child inside you, weighed down with shame, anger and tears, carrying someone else's poisonous emotional baggage. There is only you who can help this inner child and only you who can help yourself. Keep in touch with your inner child's courage which glows like an eternal flame and go on with the battle for your life.

Questioning The Past

The questions listed below are neither meant to be comprehensive nor necessarily applicable to everyone who is co-dependent, an

abuse survivor or an addict. Most of all, these questions are to help
you think, feel and remember and to connect. Write down your
answers or thoughts to the questions.

1. Do you remember your childhood before the age of 13?
   Before the age of eight? Before the age of five?
2. Can you think of 20 events, roughly one for every year of
   your life, that were emotionally intense for you from birth to
   age 20? Is this from your own recall, from a dream or from
   something that has been told to you? (Parental separation,
   physical abuse, sexual abuse, other traumatic events.)
3. Were your grandparents involved in your life in your infancy or in your childhood, either in a positive or a negative
   manner?
4. Did your grandparents live with you and your family when
   you were a child?
5. Did one or both of your grandparents drink alcohol or
   seem intoxicated when you were a child? How did they
   behave towards you?
6. Did your grandfather or grandmother physically abuse you?
   Did they beat you, choke you, slap you? Did they threaten
   you with physical punishment?
7. Did your grandfather expose himself to you when you were
   a child? Did he make you touch him? Did he put his penis
   in your mouth? Did he touch you between your legs?
8. Did your grandmother give you enemas, "clean you" in your
   genital areas when you were a child, put things inside your
   vagina or rectum?
9. Did you have any secrets with your grandparents that you
   were not allowed to tell your mother and father?
10. Did your grandfather (or grandmother) give you intoxicating
    substances? Did they do anything of a sexual kind to you
    after giving you alcohol or drugs?
11. Were either of your parents abused by their parents?
12. Do you know how your parents got together, i.e., did they
    fall in love when they were in high school or were they
    introduced by common friends?
13. Were either of your parents abused by family members
    other than parents, for example, aunts, uncles, cousins or
    their parents, boyfriends, girlfriends or step-parents?
14. Was your father supportive of your mother during the time
    that she became pregnant with you?

15. Was your father physically present while your mother was carrying you? Was he physically or emotionally abusive to your mother while she was carrying you?
16. Did your parents plan to have you? Did they think of a name for you before you were born? Were they exicted about your being born?
17. Did your mother use drugs or alcohol during her pregnancy?
18. Were your maternal grandparents supportive of your mother while she was pregnant with you?
19. Did your mother have hyperemesis gravidarum (excessive nausea and vomiting), severe weight gain, bleeding or other complications during pregnancy?
20. Did your mother attempt to abort you?
21. Did your mother ever tell you that you were a mistake?
22. Did you mother ever tell you that she wished that she had used birth control pills?
23. Are you adopted? Do you know your biologic father? Do you know your biologic mother?
24. Were you ever placed in foster homes after you were given up for adoption?
25. Were you ever placed in a foster home during times when your mother or father were separated, even for brief periods of time?
26. Were you ever placed in the care of extended family members, such as grandparents, aunts, uncles or other relatives or friends of the family for brief or extended periods of time when your parents were going through difficulties such as emotional problems, marital problems and physical illnesses? Were you physically, mentally or sexually abused during these times? What do you remember about these periods?
27. Were there any complications during childhood that may have caused injury to your body and brain and hampered your development and later caused problems with bonding between you and your mother, i.e., a cord around your neck, complicated breech, or forceps delivery?
28. Did you have any problems right after birth, for example, neonatal jaundice, convulsions, severe fevers or bleeding from the gut?
29. Were you breast fed or bottle fed?
30. If you were breast fed, was it stopped suddenly or were you weaned off gradually? If it was stopped suddenly, why?

31. Did your father support your mother's breast-feeding you or did it create problems such as her not being sexually available or her breasts becoming unattractive?
32. Were you born premature? If so, were you in intensive care for an extended period of time, separated from your mother with the possibility that you had problems bonding with her?
33. Did your mother feel that you "bonded well" or does she describe you as being difficult and fussy?
34. Was she depressed during the time that you were born? Did she suffer from clinical postpartum depression?
35. Did your mother have any major losses around the time that you were born? For example, death of a parent, separation or divorce?
36. Was she under any major stress during the time that she had you, i.e., geographic relocation, desertion by husband or physical abuse?
37. Were you colicky, did you cry excessively, did you have any feeding problems or were you severely constipated?
38. Were you removed from your parents' custody when you were an infant or a child? If so, why?
39. Were you placed in one or more foster homes as an infant or a child or a teenager? Were you physically, mentally or sexually abused in these settings? Did you see anyone being physically, mentally or sexually abused within these settings? Did any of your siblings tell you about being physically, mentally or sexually abused in foster home settings?
40. Did you have any problems rolling over, sitting up, standing up or walking and talking as a developing child?
41. What were the sleeping arrangements of your childhood? Did you sleep alone? Did you sleep with siblings? Did you share beds with older relatives of the same sex or opposite sex, such as cousins, grandparents or uncles?
42. As a child or an infant, did you have problems such as sleep-walking, head-banging, night terrors, bed-wetting or soiling when awake or sleeping?
43. Were you hyperactive when you entered school? Did you take any medications for hyperactivity?
44. Were you considered autistic when you were a child?
45. Did you have learning disabilities? Did you have problems in school?

46. Were you given enemas or threatened with being given enemas at home by your parents or step-parents?
47. Do you have older or younger siblings?
48. Did you hurt, attempt to hurt, think of hurting or killing your siblings? Were you afraid that they might hurt or kill you?
49. Were you extremely jealous of your siblings?
50. Were you sexually molested by an older sibling or their friends?
51. Did you sexually molest your younger siblings?
52. Did you masturbate for long periods of time as a child and feel tremendous guilt about such masturbation?
53. Were you punished (beaten, tied up, hands held out to a fire, matches or cigarettes or threatened to have your penis cut off) for masturbating?
54. Were you beaten, slapped around, hit with a fist, given black eyes, locked in closets, choked, had your head held under water or in a toilet as punishment for being "bad." Were you ever physically lifted off the ground by an adult or thrown across the room?
55. Did you know why you were told that you were "bad?"
56. Did you know why you got punished? Sometimes? Never?
57. Did you have caretakers other than parents, and if so, were you emotionally, physically or sexually abused or tortured by your caretakers or their boyfriends or girlfriends?
58. Did you ever have to take care of your younger brothers and sisters?
59. Did you physically or sexually molest your younger brothers or sisters while they were under your care? How did you deal with this? Did you talk to anybody about this?
60. Did your parents fight?
61. Did you see your mother being beaten by your father, step-father or her boyfriend as a child or an infant?
62. Did you see your mother being hit with fists, threatened with a knife or gun, thrown across the room, choked or strangled?
63. Did you hear your mother scream in terror and, if so, how did you react?
64. Did your mother cling to you when she was frightened?
65. Did she hold you in front of her when your father, stepfather or her boyfriend would attack her?
66. Did you try to protect your mother from being hit by your father, stepfather or your mother's boyfriend? Did you try to

console her after she was beaten? What were your feelings towards her (pity, hate, fear)?

67. Did you hear your father, stepfather or your mother's boyfriend use sexually explicit, abusive language like "bitch," "whore," or "cunt" towards your mother in your presence? How did you react? Did you feel afraid? Did you feel violent towards them? Did you feel like killing them?

68. Did your mother separate from your father when you were a child or an infant? Do you know why? How did you react? *Did* you react?

69. Were you sexually preoccupied, compulsively engaging in masturbating or inserting objects into your vagina or rectum at any period in your life as an infant, child or an adolescent?

70. Were you accident-prone as a child?

71. Were you beaten in infancy or childhood by either parent or step-parent to the point where you had black eyes or broken bones requiring one or more visits to an emergency room? Did you feel that you had to protect your parents or keep this a secret?

72. Did your parents threaten to leave you as a child because you were "bad?"

73. Were you exposed to explicit sexual activity by your parents or step-parents?

74. Have you ever watched your mother being forced to give sex or being raped?

75. Were you fondled, orally copulated, sodomized, seduced or forced to provide oral copulation by parents or step-parents?

76. Did a parent, step-parent, mother's boyfriend, uncle, grandparent or older cousin expose themselves consciously to you or masturbate in your presence or get you to masturbate them when you were an infant, child or teenager?

77. Were you witness to much violence at home? Were the police, other family members or neighbors brought in to intervene? Did this happen once or many times?

78. Did your parents drink excessively? Was it often? Was it daily? Did it create problems at work? Did either of your parents get fired because of a drinking problem? Were either sent to jail because of a drinking problem?

79. Did the drinking cause arguments or violence at home? Did it cause the police to come to your home?

80. Did your parents' drinking cause them to become "different" (violent, silly, comical, tearful, isolative, psychotic or sexualized)?

81. Did one or both parents' drinking or drug abuse make you unhappy? Did it make you unhappy to the point of feeling suicidal or wanting to run away from home?

82. Did the violence between your parents, the drinking and arguing, cause you to be unable to sleep or feel fearful? Did you feel that your mother may be hurt or killed during the time that you went to sleep?

83. Were you afraid to the point that you could not eat or ate excessively because of the fear that you experienced at home?

84. Were you scared for your mother's physical safety when your father, stepfather or mother's boyfriend got drunk or "loaded" on drugs?

85. Did your mother use pills to calm herself down?

86. Do you remember your mother being sick a lot, lying in bed for long periods of time and being emotionally and physically unavailable to you in childhood? Did she always complain of aches and pains, including headaches?

87. Did your mother confide in you as a child, constantly telling you negative things about your father? Did she confide in how she wanted to leave him and then not leave him? Did she complain about his drinking but then say nothing to him?

88. Did your mother "bad-mouth" your father or your stepfather and then spend the rest of the evening drinking with him and joking with him, leaving you puzzled and confused?

89. Did your mother ever talk to you about wanting to kill your father or your stepfather? Did she ever try to enlist you in wanting to kill your father or your stepfather? Did you feel that because you loved her you needed to help her? Did you feel guilty for not doing so or did you feel guilty for not protecting her?

90. Did your family have lots of friends and relatives who drank heavily in your presence? Did their behavior frighten you (the things that they said and did)?

91. Did they "mess" with you, as in tease you, bully you, threaten you, torture you, tickle you, fondle you?

92. Did they expose themselves, behave in a sexually explicit manner in front of you when they were intoxicated? Did they attempt to, or actually, sexually molest you?

93. Were your parents witness to any of this? What was their reaction? Did they have any reaction?

94. Did you confide in your parents about their friends mistreating you sexually or physically or making them have secrets

with you? If you did, how did your parents react? Did they show outrage? Did they act to stop it? Did their friends continue to visit even after you told them that you were uncomfortable or that you were being abused? Were you disbelieved or your story discounted or laughed at? Was it minimized or trivialized?

95. Have you been raped as a child or an adolescent? Do you think about the rape? Do you have flashbacks about the rape? Do you try not to think about the rape?

96. What feelings do you have connected to the rape when you think about it or try not to think about it? Anger/rage, fear, paranoia? Anxiety panic? Sexual excitement? Hopelessness and wanting to die? Homicidal feelings? Thoughts of emasculating (mutilating the genitals) the rapist?

97. If you were raped in childhood or adolescence, were you anally and/or orally raped. How was it? Was it confined to vaginal intercourse? Did the rapist involve more than one person? Did the rapist or rapists masturbate on you? Did they call you names? What kind of names did they call you? Did they tell you that they knew you liked it?

98. Were bondage, physical beatings, being held at knifepoint or gunpoint a part of the rape trauma?

99. Were you intoxicated when you were raped? Were you coerced to take alcohol or drugs prior to being raped? Was the rapist intoxicated?

100. Did the rapist threaten to kill you or your family members if you disclosed what happened?

101. Did you disclose to family members? Did you disclose to friends? Did your family bring it to the attention of the police?

102. Do you have dreams about having been raped in childhood?

103. Were you raped more than once by the same person?

104. How do you feel about the person who raped you at this time?

105. Were you reminded often in interactions with others about the rapist (when you interacted with other people's parents, brothers or people who worked around you or knew your family members)? Did you avoid activities such as going to school, avoid people because of your fear that you might be raped again?

106. Did you come away with the feeling that you were a good person or that you were a bad person or did you not feel either because of your rape?

107. Did you have to appear in court to testify against a person who raped you or molested you in childhood? What were your feelings about that? How did your parents support you or not support you during this time?

108. Did your family members continue to encourage you to talk about the rape or did they encourage you *not* to talk about the rape? Did they seem to not want to discuss it again or did they actively inquire if you were still bothered by what had happened?

109. Did you get pregnant by incest or rape when you were a teenager? Did you disclose the pregnancy to your parents? Did you disclose the pregnancy to anyone? Did you abort it on your own? Did you obtain an illegal abortion? Did you allow the pregnacy to continue to term? Did you keep the child? Did you give up the child for adoption?

110. Have you ever become pregnant by a parent, step-parent or a sibling, uncle or grandparent having sex with you? What feelings did you have at the time? What was the reaction of your family members? What are your reactions now? How do you feel about your family members now?

111. Did your teachers, either in grade school, kindergarten or high school, become involved with you sexually? What was the nature of sexual contact at the time? Was it heterosexual or homosexual contact? How did you react when it happened? How did you react after it happened? Was it a single incident or was it multiple incidents spread out over a period of time?

112. Were you sexually abused by any other figure in authority such as a priest? A probation officer? A policeman? While you were a teenager? How did you react to being abused at the time? Did you think about it or did you block it out? Did you talk to your family members about it? Did you receive support from them or did they disbelieve you? If they believed you, did they make inquiries and take action?

113. Have you been sexually molested or raped by a counselor or a therapist when you were a child or a teenager? This includes being touched in the breast and genital areas, being kissed on the mouth or being made to touch the person's genital area, i.e., breasts, groin or lips. How did you react at

the time. Did you feel that you were special? Did you feel that you were being taken advantage of? Did you talk to anyone about it?

114. Did you ever run away from home because you were forced to have sex with family members, including siblings, parents or step-parents or grandparents? How were you responded to? Were you able to contact authorities? Did they act to protect you? How do you feel towards your family members who may have abused you during that time? What is your current relationship with family members who were present when the abuse took place?

115. Do you think about your childhood as being primarily un-happy (sad, gloomy, suicidal, hopeless, helpless), happy/joyful or neutral, generally speaking?

116. How do your remember Christmases, New Year's Days, your birthdays and the weekends and your vacations during your childhood days? Was there a lot of drinking during these occasions? Did this drinking lead up to fights, physical abuse, verbal abuse, sexual abuse of family disruption to the point of neighbors being involved or the police being called?

117. Did you have imaginary companions of a positive or a negative type when you were lonely? Did you talk to them when no one else was around and seem to hear them talk to you when you were a child? Would you hide up in attics, closets, under the bed or in corners in the room or find other hideaway spots to daydream and get away?

118. Were you lonely a lot?

119. Were you bored a lot in your childhood and adolescence?

120. Did you prefer to be away from home (i.e., at school or at friends' homes) as opposed to being at home with your parents or siblings?

121. Did you think of being dead? A little? A lot? Do you remem-ber times when you felt very strongly about wanting to be dead? Can you relate it to any incident or incidents in your life? Did you try to kill yourself? Once? More than once?

122. Did you think once or on many occasions about how your family members would feel about your being dead? Did you visualize your being dead? Did you visualize yourself in a coffin? Did you visualize your family members around you at your funeral? Did you think about how your mother, your father, your brothers, your grandparents and other people

involved in your life would react to it? Did you do this a little or a lot?

123. Did you spend time imagining how sorry your parents would be when you were dead?

124. Did you feel angry a lot? Did you feel rage to a degree that you would hit your fist on the wall, cut yourself, hit your head with your fists or call yourself stupid?

125. Did you wish your father, your stepfather or your mother or your stepmother dead? A little? A lot? Can you relate it to specific incidents? Did you feel guilty at such thoughts? Did you wish you were dead because you had these thoughts? Did you think that you would go to hell for having these thoughts? Have you ever had a chance to tell them the way you felt? How do you think they would have responded?

126. Do you remember your parents separating or divorcing? Did you know why they separated? How did you react to their separation? Did you feel angry, guilty, sad or scared? Were you glad that they separated?

127. Did you blame yourself for your parents separating? Did they tell you that it was your fault? Did they tell you that it was *not* your fault? Did they prepare you for it, such as by sitting down and talking to you? Was it well planned or was it abrupt? Did it happen after an incident of drinking and violence?

128. Did your father (or mother) continue to visit you and be involved with you after your parents separated?

129. Were you emotionally abused, put down, shamed, cursed, beaten physically or sexually abused by your mother, your father, your stepfather or your stepmother or your mother's boyfriend during these visits? Did you tell your custodial parent about the abuse? What was the response of your custodial parent upon being told about how you were being treated by the noncustodial parent?

130. Did either of your parents tell you once or more than once that if it were not for you they would not want to continue living? How did you respond? What were your feelings when they told you this? Did you feel sad for them? Did you feel angry with them? Did you feel that you were important? Did you feel that it was a burden on you? Did you worry about them being dead or killing themselves? Did you think about it a little or were you obsessed about them killing themselves?

131. Did you feel compelled to comfort your father or stepfather by providing sex because he made you feel sorry for him

for the way your mother treated him? What were your feelings at the time that it happened? What were your feelings
when you thought about it afterwards? What are your feelings at this time about the incident? What are your feelings
towards your family members who were there at the time
when this happened?

132. Were you compelled to give sex to your stepfather or your
mother's boyfriend so they would not hurt your mother?

133. Did your father, stepfather or mother's boyfriend, uncle, cousin or family friend threaten to kill you, your mother or your
siblings if you told on them about their sexual secrets, i.e.,
their molesting you? Did they ever threaten to kill your pet?
Did they kill a pet or another animal in front of you to make
an example of what would happen to you?

134. Did your father, stepfather or mother's boyfriend threaten to
kill themselves or leave your mother if you told on them?

135. Were you given money or candy for keeping secrets about
sexual participation with older adults? How did you feel
about it at the time? How do you feel about it now?

136. Were you ever involved, as far back as you can remember
(either from memories, dreams, flashbacks, or from stigmata[1]), in Satan worship, ritual abuse, voodoo or cultic
involvement, including break-away sections from the Ma-
sons, Campus Crusade for Christ and any other religious and
quasi-religious organization?

137. Did you participate in chanting or the ritual killing of animals during these times? When you have flashbacks of these,
do you feel faint? Do you feel like your heart is going to
stop? Have you actually fainted or thrown up?

138. Have you participated in the sacrifice of infants? Do you
remember how you felt then? If you remember, what are
your feelings about it now?

139. Were you forced to eat animals that were sacrificed or drink
their blood?

140. Were you involved in cannibalism during these rituals? Were
you forced to drink human blood?

141. Have you ever had pictures of you taken without your
clothes on by adults? Were you told that you were a "movie
star" or a "model?" Were you made to behave in a sexually
explicit manner by adults in such a way that you were
caught between getting so much attention and feeling important, and then believing that it was too late to be able to

get out of it, feeling trapped and scared that it was not "okay?" Were you given money, gifts or toys to participate in such activities? Were you threatened to be hurt or killed or have people close to you hurt or killed if you talked?

142. Did you masturbate as a child or a teenager? Did you masturbate to such a degree that you were constantly preoccupied by it (several times a day)? Did you feel dirty or disgusted with yourself after you masturbated? What would you fantasize about during the time that you masturbated?

143. Did masturbation involve putting objects inside your vagina or rectum? Did you ever put dangerous objects such as knives or other potentially injurious articles inside your vagina or rectum? Did you involve yourself in masturbation that caused pain? What were your feelings about it at the time that it happened? What are your feelings about it now?

144. Did the people who molested you as a child put things inside your vagina or rectum? What were your feelings about it then? What are your feelings about it now? How do you feel towards the people who did this to you?

145. Did your preoccupation with masturbation and masturbating cause you to feel that you were bad to the point that you thought of killing yourself because you were such a bad person?

146. Were you ever caught masturbating by your parent or stepparent? Did they ever threaten that you would go to hell for doing this? Did they tell you that you were bad? Did they ever flick a finger on your penis when you had an erection?

147. When did you first become sexually involved? With a same-age partner? With older boys and girls? With men and women?

148. How did your father or stepfather deal with finding out that you were dating someone? How did they treat the other person, i.e., your boyfriend? Your girlfriend?

149. Did your parent or step-parent "come on" sexually to your friends? How did you feel about it?

150. Did you seem to be more sexually aware and active than most people in your peer group? How did you acquire your knowledge about sexual activity? Did you obtain it from your friends? Relatives? Your parents? From magazines, books and films?

151. Did you involve yourself sexually with men who were much older, i.e., in their 20s, 30s, 40s and 50s, when you were 10 to 14 years old?

152. How did you feel about it at the time? Did you feel special?
Did you feel that they were more protective? Were you afraid
of them? How do you feel about it now?

153. Were these relationships with older men under coercion,
threats or being seduced by gifts or protection?

154. Did you feel disturbed about being gay or not being sure
about your sexual identity to the point of feeling seriously
depressed, confused, anxious and suicidal? Did you desire
to be of the opposite sex? Did you know why? Did you talk
to anyone about it? How did they respond?

155. Did you overeat or become fat as a child or a teenager just
around the time that you approached puberty?

156. Did you eat large amounts of sweets and starchy food
alone, in hiding? Did you stuff away large amounts of food
under your bed or in other places where you could reach
it and other people did not know about it? Did you eat in
the bathroom? Would you bring yourself to vomit after
you overate?

157. Did you have any difficulties in school? Were you hyperactive? Were you reprimanded for "daydreaming?" Were you
"spacy?" Were you preoccupied by sexual, violent or suicidal
thoughts while in school to a degree that it began to affect
your education?

158. Have you ever thought of or attempted suicide? Once? Or
many times, in childhood? How did you think about killing
yourself? Did you think about killing yourself by hanging?
Overdosing? Cutting your wrists? Jumping off the top of a
building? Running in front of a truck or car? How did you
come to decide upon the way in which you wanted to kill
yourself? Did you know anyone that had killed themselves
in a similar way? Within the family? Outside of the family?
Did you get the idea about how you would kill yourself
from reading books? Magazines? TV?

159. Did you remember any event in your childhood in which
someone killed themselves or you read about it (i.e., hearing
about a child or a teenager who was going through circum-
stances similar to yours) and it triggered off your own
thoughts about wanting to be dead?

160. Did you hear voices, including those telling you that you
were bad or you were a slut? Was it your own voice? Have
you heard moaning or whimpering or heard a child's voice
inside you? Did you hear angry voices and "put-downs" of

adult men and women, possibly family members, when you were a child?

161. Were you raped as a child or an adolescent? Once? Multiple times? Were you gang raped? Were you date raped? Were you intoxicated while you were sexually molested or raped? Did you tell anyone about the rape? How did you think they were going to react to it?

162. Did you do sexual favors to same-age or older boys and girls so that they would like you?

163. Did you contract venereal diseases? How did you react to it at the time? Were you afraid? Did you think of killing yourself? Did you talk to anyone about it? How did your doctor react when you told him about it? How did your parents react when you talked to them about it?

164. Did you run away from home? Why? What were your feelings at the time towards your parents? What was your parents' reaction?

165. Did you get into trouble with the law as a teenager, for breaking and entering, for shoplifting, for selling drugs, for violent behavior or for engaging in prostitution?

166. When did you first use drugs or alcohol? Did your father or stepfather, mother or stepmother give it to you? Did your siblings give it to you? Did extended family members (uncles, cousins, grandparents) give it to you? Did any of these people sexually involve you while your were intoxicated?

167. Did you do drugs or alcohol on a daily or regular basis? Did you stay "loaded" while you were at home and/or at school? Did your involvement with drugs cause you to drop out of school, become truant, cause you to drop out of sports?

168. Did your involvement with drugs and alcohol cause you to change from one peer group to another peer group, even though you had some negative feelings about your drug abusing peer group?

169. Did you sell drugs or give sexual favors for drugs or alcohol when you were a child or a teenager?

170. Did you suffer blackouts with drugs?

171. Did you suffer blackouts without drugs?

172. Did you engage in prostitution? Was it one time or was it many times? Did it involve a time when you were using drugs? Did it involve a time when you had run away from home?

173. Were you sexually abused, raped, beaten or tortured by a pimp?
174. Did you feel like you were more than one person? Have you every felt like there are two or more very different personalities within yourself, each of which is dominant at a particular time? Did you feel that the diffferent "persons" have different names, clothes, attitudes, feelings and ways of thinking, sometimes one totally opposite to the other?
175. Did you feel these different personalities talking among themselves or arguing among themselves inside your head?
176. Did you feel disconnected from your body? Did you feel numb? Did you feel like a "watcher" in your own life? Did you feel like you were an automaton (robot-like)?
177. Have you had migraines, pelvic problems, endometriosis, severe pain with menstruation? Have you had problems such as irritable bowel syndrome (colitis) as a child? Did you have fainting spells? Did you have panic attacks with flashbacks of abuse where you felt difficulty in breathing, a choking sensation, gasping and having uncomfortable sensations, including tightness of the chest, cringing of the skin? Did you feel uncomfortable sensations around your breast and genital area? When would these happen? Would certain family members or extended family members precipitate such feelings?
178. Have these happened at nighttime when you have awakened suddenly or when you were alone?
179. Have you engaged in binging and purging behaviors?

All of the above questions deal with painful feelings and some are "unthinkable" thoughts that you have struggled not to be aware of, secrets that you have blotted out of your mind so you can protect some family members.

Yet awareness is a necessary first step towards recovery. If you don't ask the questions, you cannot begin to think and if you don't think, you cannot begin to work through. Painful as it may be, it is part of inventory taking, part of reaching out to your inner child.

So, like the parent it never had, you can ask and you can listen and be the adult to your inner child who can then begin to let go of its fear, sadness, hoplessness and guilt. And most of all, you will begin to connect even as an adult to some of the *courage* of your childhood, and this will help you every day.

Once again, exercising, massaging yourself, taking soothing baths and other calming activities, taking the time to play, holding onto positive people in your life (spouse, friends, therapists, sponsors) will help. These include physically holding onto them at times or being held by them when you read these questions. Back off if you feel physically sick. Use your self-soothing skills to calm down and then go back to it.

Recovery comes at a cost. It is a childlike mentality, so common among addicts and co-dependents, that sometimes creates the expectation that recovery will happen "one fine day." Recovery is a process and especially in the early stages, every day, every hour, every moment might seem torturous. But there are no shortcuts. This is the battle for your life.

---

1. Stigmata are bodily signs of ritual abuse including carving or burning occult and Satanic symbols on the person.

SIX

Characteristics Of Co-dependents, Addicts And Adult Children of Dysfunctional Families

Slaves lose everything in their chains, even the desire of escaping them.

Rousseau

People who grow up in dysfunctional, abusive, discounting and shaming homes with alcoholic and chemically dependent parents act, think and feel in ways strongly influenced by their childhoods. Even when they have no memory of the storms and the violence and the daily horror of their youth, the manner in which they live their lives out screams out their secret pain — pain which does not allow them to reach their full potential as people.

The characteristics of co-dependents, addicts and abuse survivors influence the way they act, the way they treat their bodies, their moods, their thoughts and their relationships.

47

Behavior is the most obvious manifestation of these characteristics. That is what bothers people most of all when it is not acceptable. You can walk around wishing you or someone else were dead, but as long as you smile and say the right things, you are of no concern to others. However, once you start *doing things*, all hell breaks loose. Throw objects, cut your wrist, beat someone up, try to balance on the Golden Gate Bridge and people will sit up and take notice.

Survivors can relate to behavior at another level. *Acting to please or displease people has been the story of their lives.* Whether it's aggressive behavior, sexualized behavior, disturbances in sleeping or eating, what is evident in the abuse survivor, the co-dependent and the addict is the problem of excesses — too much, too little, deviant or inconsistent.

For the addict/co-dependent/survivor, actions and behavior take place as a knee-jerk reflex, without reflection. Often they act on feelings of the false self. A false self that acts in rage, shame, fear and foolish self-defeating pride, a false self that is disconnected from their own inner courage.

Bob, a heroin addict, suffered from terrifying anxiety attacks. I recommended that he exercise. In spite of my reassurance that everything was fine with his heart, he could not get himself to exercise because when he felt his heart pounding, he *felt* he was going to die. I literally had to take him by the hand and run along-side him to fight the childish fear.

Barbara, a bright, educated woman, felt that her husband would always hurt her and this was her reason for an ongoing abusive marriage. Years of growing up with an abusive father and a co-dependent mother had conditioned her to feel this way. She was not able to "talk herself out of it," even though she read endless numbers of self-help books and attended many self-help lectures.

Co-dependents and addicts have tremendous problems with behaviors. Either they have problems in taking any kind of action and their lives are stuck because of their tremendous passivity or they act in impulsive, explosive or compulsive manners. What is difficult for the co-dependent is *decisive action-taking,* whether it is completing their schooling or getting a restraining order or taking the time to be good to themselves.

The basic disturbances involve instinctual drive behaviors— *aggression, sexuality, sleeping* and *feeding.*

A self-test can help you recognize if there is a disturbance. All items are scored:

Never = 0
Once, sometimes = 1
Often = 2
Always = 3

A Self Test: Aggressive Behaviors

1. Do you have outbursts of violent behavior?
2. Have you destroyed property during periods of violent behavior?
3. Have you beaten your spouse, child or parents, once or repeatedly?
4. Is violence a part of your sexual activity (bondage, rape, sadomasochism)?
5. Have you physically beaten or injured an animal?
6. Have you ever been charged with assault and battery?

Items 7-10 suggest failure of normal aggressive instinct:

7. Have you been beaten as an adult?
8. Have you been repeatedly beaten by the same person (other than a parent)?
9. Have you ever been raped?
10. Have you ever been in a relationship which is frequently violent, with you as the victim?

A Self-Test: Sexual Dysfunction

1. Has your sexual behavior caused you trouble with your loved ones or society?
2. Have you committed rape?
3. Do you feel aroused too much of the time to a level where it disrupts your work and your social life?
4. Have you engaged in or thought about engaging in prostitution?
5. Have you engaged in or thought about engaging in sadomasochistic sex?
6. Have you engaged in sexual deviant behavior such as sex with children (pedophilia), sex involving violence (beating or being beaten), cross-dressing, enema fetish, sex with animals, voyeurism (peeping Tom), making lewd phone calls, exhibitionism ("flasher") or being excited by playing with urine and/or feces?

7. Have you often or always had a problem not getting sexually aroused?
8. Are you often or always unable to obtain an erection or maintain it?
9. Have you sustained injury to your genitals because of excessive masturbation?
10. Have you mutilated your genitals as part of sexual excitement?
11. Are you able to have orgasms?
12. Do you have problems with premature ejaculation?
13. Do you have pain after or during sexual intercourse?
14. Do you suffer from vaginismus (involuntary spasm of the musculature of the outer third of the vagina) that interferes with intercourse?
15. Have you been or are you impotent?
16. Have you been or are you at the present time frigid?

Healthy sexual functioning depends upon a healthy childhood and infantile development. This is the reason why sex therapy can never be an isolated treatment. My sense is that this is the reason why the "miraculous cures" of Masters and Johnson and others have not withstood the passage of time.

Sexual problems don't take place at the level of the groin. Sexual problems take place in the mind. Sexual problems should compel you to take an inventory of the self.

A Self Test: Disturbances Of Eating Behaviors In Co-dependents, Addicts And Abuse Survivors

A. Too Much

1. Do you engage in binge eating—rapidly consuming large amounts of high calorie, often sweet food that can be eaten easily, like donuts, candy, bread and cakes?
2. Do you eat large amounts of food in secret?
3. Does your excessive eating affect your social life, your sleep or your physical health? Does it cause pain and/or vomiting?
4. Have you ever been 30 pounds heavier than what is acceptable for your height?

B. Too Little

5. Have you engaged in periods of self-starvation?
6. Have you lost one-fourth or over 30 pounds of what is an acceptable weight for yourself?

7. Have you engaged in self-starvation to the point that you have stopped having menstrual periods?
8. Have you ever been hospitalized for the medical complications of self-starvation?
9. Do you or have you induced vomiting?
10. Have you used large amounts of laxatives to lose weight?
11. Have you exercised to such a degree purely to lose weight, even though you are not overweight as told by your doctors?
12. Are you obsessed with the kind of food that you eat, including preoccupation with food allergies and constant concerns about how it will affect you? Are you preoccupied with problems of "hypoglycemia?" Are you constantly preoccupied by feeling that the foods you eat on a day-to-day basis that most people eat will poison you?
13. Do you seem to be chronically preoccupied with what you eat, even though you eat very little and have a hard time putting on any weight?

My experience is that most people who have eating disorders come from enmeshed/abusive/neglectful families. I have seen many incest and ritual abuse survivors who went from therapist to therapist and were diagnosed as having an "eating disorder."

Not getting to the roots, i.e., the abuse trauma, is the cause of relapse for people who are treated in eating disorder programs. You have to treat the cause, even while you treat the effects.

A Self Test: Disturbances Of Sleeping Behavior

As Nietzsche said, *"Sleeping is no mean art: for its sake one must stay awake all day."* Sleep also is the foundation of good health. It regulates the nervous, endocrine and immune systems. People who grow up in unstable and abusive families have poorly developed sleep mechanisms. Some of the sleep problems that should make you suspicious of abuse are the following (once again, a high score suggests a strong need for memory work and inventory-taking of childhood:

1. Does it take you an hour or longer to fall asleep?
2. Do you wake up frequently (post-traumatic stress disorder type of sleep disturbance)?
3. Do you have difficulty falling asleep (anxiety type of sleep disorder)?

4. Do you wake up at 1:00 or 2:00 or 3:00 in the morning, several hours before your normal waking up time and find it difficult to fall asleep (depression type of sleep pattern)?
5. Do you feel well rested on waking up or do you feel mentally and physically fatigued?
6. Do you have nightmares, sweating and startled awakening frequently?
7. Do you sleep excessively, i.e., 9-15 hours a day, and still get the feeling that you have not slept enough?
8. Have you used or do you use sleeping pills such as Halcion, Dalmane, chloral hydrate, Valium, Xanax or Librium to help you sleep? Have you used alcohol or marijuana to help you sleep?
9. Have you had problems with sleep-walking, thrashing around in your sleep or becoming violent in your sleep?
10. Do you wet your bed presently or have you wet your bed as an adult?
11. Do you have periods of time when you feel that you cannot wake up from bed and you feel paralyzed in your sleep?

If you have scored high or very high on the self-test, it is an indication that there is a serious problem in your life and you need to attend to it. No matter if you tell yourself that you have a nice job and that this new guy that you met is really cute—there is a problem if eating, sleeping, aggressive and sexual behavior is affected. You need to take a look at your life.

SEVEN

Assault On The Self: Suicide, Self-Mutilation And Self-Destructive Lifestyles

*Whatever crazy sorrow saith no life that breathes
with human breath has ever truly longed for death.*

Lord Tennyson

Suicide has a wide range of meanings for the survivor, the addict and the co-dependent. Many co-dependents attempt and complete suicides. Suicide is very high among alcoholics and drug addicts even after they have given up their primary addictions.

Suicidal behaviors and thoughts of suicide are universally present among adults who have been abused as children. Why is this so?

Parental Loss And Suicide

Parental loss corrolates strongly with suicide. A child can lose a parent through death. A child also can lose a parent through separation and divorce where one parent is no longer actively present in the picture. A child can lose a parent when this parent no longer functions as a parent, as in the role reversal seen in parents who are constantly dysfunctional and children who are "parentalized." The child loses a parent when the parent no longer functions as a parent as when he or she sexually abuses the child.

When a father or stepfather becomes a child's sexual lover, the child in essence loses the parent. Various degrees of abandonment and loss are felt when parental functions of protection, love, adoration and consistency go unfulfilled.

People from broken homes are five times as vulnerable to suicide as those from intact homes. Adult children of alcoholics are more likely to come from broken homes. And even when the family is seemingly intact, the parents are so wrapped up in their own problems that the children feel emotionally abandoned and sense the loss which sets them up to feel the self-hate — which sets them up for suicide later in life.

The common purpose of suicide is to seek a solution. The common emotion of suicide is hopelessness and helplessness. The thinking of a suicidal person is one of constriction and seeing no other alternatives. Suicide can be attention-seeking, driven by rage and anger and the need to provoke guilt in others.

For co-dependents, addicts and abuse survivors, all of these items are true.

Suicidal Thoughts As Self-Empowerment

From an early age, a child from a dysfunctional family thinks of suicide as an alternative, one of the very few choices that they truly have. For someone who has nothing that is truly theirs, the capacity to take their own life and inflict wounds on their own body is an ace in their deck of cards.

In my experience, adult children of alcoholic families have spent long periods of childhood—days, weeks and months—alone, hiding in their rooms, trying to sleep and not being able to sleep and staring at the ceiling, feeling the coldness, the hate and the fear around them, feeling suicidal, contemplating various ways of killing themselves, fantasizing, planning, ruminating—hour after hour, day after day, thinking how it will affect themselves and others.

This may have been a "safety valve" which paradoxically allowed them to live through the day and make it through the night.

Vanessa, for example, grew up in rural Texas. Her father, an alcoholic, abandoned the family when she was three years old. The mother was overwhelmed with the caretaking and sent the child to Vanessa's aunt. Life between age four and ten consisted of doing housework for her alcoholic aunt and her aunt's alcoholic boyfriend. She was beaten regularly by both of them.

She was also sexually abused. The abuse included being forced to bend over the bed with her buttocks thrust up, her legs spread to expose her genitals. She would be struck repeatedly by her aunt's boyfriend on her buttocks and on her genitals, as her aunt and her boyfriend would laugh hysterically, curse her, call her a whore and a slut and make jokes about her "pussy." (All this happened at age six.)

She would be beaten more if she screamed. She learned to "go away" (dissociate). Initially she would get shaky in her legs, scream and lose control of her bladder (for which she would be beaten even more). Besides taunting her, the aunt would force open her genitals and the boyfriend would put the handle of a bullwhip, as well as his penis, into the child's vagina and rectum. At other times, the aunt's boyfriend would be "nice" to her, buy her ice cream or give her petty cash as rewards for sexual favors. Vanessa told me that she believed that her aunt did this so that "her man would not stray away from her."

She dealt with these multiple traumas in many ways. She would deal with her rage by catching rats, tying wire to their tails and burning them slowly over a grill, imagining that it was her aunt and her boyfriend who were being fried. She would hear the shrieks and make believe that it was her aunt and her aunt's boyfriend who were screaming for mercy. She would sometimes feel guilty about killing the mice. (Later in life, her tremendous rage caused her to inflict physical abuse on her seven children.)

She would initiate oral and genital sex with her younger brother and then she would feel guilty. She would sob into her pillow and stare at the willow tree outside her window, and see herself hanging from the bough. Later she would imagine a dark shadow that would come from the tree to "take her away."

As an adult, in spite of being bright and hardworking, with many compulsive skills, she has shown little success coping at work and has been regularly abused at work by her bosses and her co-workers who loaded her up with other people's work. Her two marriages have both been to substance-abusing, physically-abusive men. She has outbursts of rage towards her children during which times she physically and emotionally abuses them. She has periods of intense paranoia and cannot bear to be alone. At the same time she cannot stand people.

She has bouts of imminent suicidal feelings with impending feelings of loss of control. These happen after fights with her children, attempts at sexual activity or after a bad dream that she wakes up from. Abuse at work drives her into suicidal states.

The patient was "addicted to suicide." She would spend large parts of her day and night contemplating suicide and in a way it would seem like an escape from other known alternatives such as leaving the job, separating from her boyfriend, placing her children for a period of time in institutions where they would be cared for and being firm with her friends and employers who abused and used her.

Triggers Affecting Self-Esteem

An abuse survivor/addict/co-dependent needs to recognize some important things about their suicidal potential. As Yogi Berra said, "It ain't over till it's over." It is the dissociated feelings (suppressed, pushed down, denied) of an agonizing, hopeless, helpless childhood that emerge into their current life. The things that trigger them may be largely unrecognized. Any trigger that affect self-esteem or self-acceptance may cause shame, guilt, unacceptable rage or uncontrollable fear. Confrontation with the boss, separation from a boyfriend, girlfriend, child, friend or parent; or a phone call or a bad dream — these can quickly build into suicidal feelings as the only way out of these feelings.

All of these can push them back from a seemingly happy, well-adjusted, confident state to an adult child feeling worthless and welling up with self-hate. Suddenly, in a matter of hours, they have no reason to live and want to die NOW.

Don't Minimize Suicidal Gestures

Subtle thoughts, attempts and gestures of suicide are serious signals of unaddressed childhood trauma and must never be minimized. They are even more serious when they come and go because they suggest that, in addition to feeling suicidal, you are disconnected from real thoughts and feelings, buried in an unhappy childhood. They call for a journey into your past, a need for inventory-taking.

Self-Mutilation

Like suicide, self-mutilation can be an attempt to express a variety of feelings:

1. Feelings of self-hate, expressed in disfiguring and causing hurt to the hated self—a self-punishment.
2. Feelings of anger, especially towards parents and parentlike figures turned toward the self.
3. A way of escaping overwhelming emotional pain and grief without killing oneself and in the absence of mind-numbing chemical addictions.
4. Self-mutilation is a way of assuring oneself of having control even if it is only the control to cut or burn oneself and "mastering the pain."
5. A fix, a "pill"—symptomatic relief for anxiety, used almost like a chemical addiction.
6. A cry for help.
7. To express anger towards the "bad parts" (self-mutilation of genitals), common among incest survivors.
8. A source of sexual excitement (genital mutilation), often seen with men and some women who habitually use pain as a way of obtaining sexual excitement.
9. A psychotic way of dealing with sexual identity confusion (genital mutilation and emasculation—cutting off the penis and/or the testicles).
10. As a way of escaping boredom.

Forms Of Self-Mutilation

1. Cutting with knives, blades, sharp paper, broken glass.
2. Burning, usually with cigarettes, sometimes with matches or a lighter and rarely, over an open fire.
3. Insertion through nipples, breasts and genitals of pins, sometimes associated with cross-dressing and partial strangulation/ suffocation and the insertion of rectal dildos for the purpose of sexual excitement in people with sexual identity problems and sadomasochistic sexual addictions.
4. Using rough surfaces such as brushes to scrape skin to the point of bleeding.
5. Picking at skin with fingernails, knives or other implements to cause pain and disfigurement.

6. Tattooing, especially with crude instruments, often rubbing ink or tobacco ash into the exposed wounds, frequently used as a way of "making a statement."

Ralph is a 30-year-old Navy veteran with a history of alcoholism, depression and bisexuality. He attempted to remove his testicles with a large knife. Working through in treatment, a childhood emerged that was enmeshed with a co-dependent mother, a father who was alcoholic and violent and who often threatened the patient that he would "cut his pecker off" as a child. In recovery, Ralph gave up his bisexuality and emerged as fully homosexual, something that he was not able to admit to himself previously.

Ramona, a 26-year-old Navy veteran, always wore full sleeves. Her entire arm from wrist to shoulder had scars, contractures and infections because of burning herself with cigarettes. She had been diagnosed previously as borderline schizophrenic. She came to recognize through treatment that she had been molested by her father, paternal grandfather and several paternal uncles, including being gang-raped by them, both as an infant and as a child.

Theresa, a 29-year-old alcoholic, was admitted because she had scraped her abdomen with a metal brush until it was completely bloody and excoriated. It happened after she moved in with her father whom she had not seen since she was six years old. Her father manipulated her into giving him sex for providing her with a place to stay. She has had a history of self-mutilation from adolescence. In therapy, she became consciously aware of her father sexually abusing her from infancy all the way through childhood before he broke up with her mother when she was six years old.

Self-mutilation may often be accomplished in a dissociated, depersonalized, trancelike state of mind, or the patient may be in a fully conscious state. Drugs and alcohol may accompany the self-mutilating process.

All self-mutilation is serious. All self-mutilation strongly suggests an abusive childhood. These behaviors are chronic and addictive and often prevent the person, just like alcohol and drugs, from seeking healthier ways towards recovery.

Self-mutilation is highest with females who have been incested by a male parent at a very early age. The incest trauma itself is usually not remembered.

Genital mutilation should raise the question of ritual abuse or violent incestuous sexual abuse.

All self-mutilation calls for inventory-taking and for memory work. Massage, while fought off by the self-mutilator, has a tremendous impact towards helping recovery.

Self-mutilators are best helped by attending Incest Survivor 12-Step meetings.

Self-Destructive Behaviors And Lifestyles

Chronic risk-taking, for example, by driving excessively fast, playing Russian roulette, taking dangerous drugs, attempting acrobatics from high places without adequate training, associating with violent peer groups, engaging in prostitution and engaging in sadomasochistic lifestyles and groups are often seen among abuse survivors, especially in the young. They are *never* seen in people who come from a well-adjusted childhood.

Such behaviors reflect a variety of feelings:

Self-hate and covert attempts to commit suicide.
Attempts to fight off chronic underlying hopelessness.
Constant need to fight underlying fear (counterphobic).
An attempt to fight off intense and overwhelming boredom.
Lack of a sense of feeling alive (getting an adrenalin rush).
Constant, often intense sense of threatened masculinity.

As with suicide and self-mutilation, self-destructive behaviors and lifestyles are a strong clue to an abusive childhood and need to be dealt with in the same manner.

EIGHT

Physical Symptoms Of Co-dependents, Addicts And Abuse Survivors

*C*hristine came to me because she had marital problems. Her husband, during the course of her 30-year marriage, had numerous affairs, including fathering a child by another woman, and wanted at this time to move out and move in with this girlfriend. Christine came to see me so that she could "save her marriage."

She had never confronted her husband about his affairs and his sexual addiction. Her own father had numerous affairs that her mother *tolerated*. "My mother was a martyr," she said.

Christine felt this was the way men treated women and this was the way women had to handle that treatment. Her own mother was chronically physically ill with headaches, continuous complaints of back pain and "female problems" but was never treated for depression.

The patient herself has had migraines, irritable bowel syndrome (colitis) and severe sleep disturbance but does not state depression as a complaint. She did not think that anything was the matter with the way she conducted her life. She felt that nothing was wrong with her.

Like so many other abuse survivors, addicts and co-dependents, Christine may not be able to see anything wrong with the way she lives her life at a conscious level. And she is not lying. They *believe* what they say.

Their bodies carry the pain of their emotional burden and cry out in the form of illnesses.

The questions listed below may give the co-dependent, the addict and the abuse survivor a clue that in fact there is something "wrong."

I started out with a physical symptoms check list after behaviors because this is the second most common way in which emotionally repressed and denied people will "complain." For a lot of women in this country, medical illnesses are the only way in which they express discontent and emotional pain. For years they often see a family practitioner who treats their headaches with Valium and their stomach upset with Maalox or Librax but never gets a whimper from the patient about her alcoholic spouse who beats her and the children every night. These are the secrets that shame them and their families. It is much easier to talk about your head hurting.

I hope that the following questions will help survivors and their loved ones spot the possibility of unresolved abuse trauma in their lives.

Along the road to recovery there are many barriers. Defenses such as amnesia (the forgetting of traumatic events), denial (an unconscious belief that the feeling and memory no longer bother you), repression (consciously pushing painful thoughts away), and acting out (engaging in often self-destructive behavior so as not to allow oneself to feel), intellectualization (coming up with adult reasons and explanations for hurts inflicted by others instead of allowing yourself to admit and feel these feelings).

These defenses call for more than just motivation, i.e., wanting to get better. Overcoming them needs knowledge, the awareness that something is wrong, maybe terribly wrong.

The Physical Symptoms of Abuse

1. Do you have unexplained periods of
   dizziness?   Yes   No

2. Do you have periods in which things become very small when you look at them or
   things become very large, i.e., hallways, fur-
   niture, as if you were looking through the
   eyes of a child?   Yes   No

3. Do you suffer from periods of unexplained blindness?   Yes No

4. Do you suffer from migraine headaches that do not seem to get relieved in spite of different medications? Migraine is described as an often one-sided headache, often having an aura, a "feeling before it starts" often accompanied by visual disturbances, nausea and an inability to tolerate light.   Yes No

5. Do you suffer from chronic tension headaches in which your forehead, the back of the neck, the back of your head and the neck area are feeling very tight but not "pounding?"   Yes No

6. Do you often suffer from burning, tingling sensations in your face and mouth (often related to hyperventilation)?   Yes No

7. Do you sometimes or often have choking sensations, difficulty swallowing (a lump in the throat) or tightness around your neck and chest?   Yes No

8. Have you had syncope episodes (fainting spells)?   Yes No

9. Do you have chest pain, pounding in the chest or pain like a "heart attack?"   Yes No

10. Do you have unexplained shortness of breath?   Yes No

11. Do you have periods of high blood pressure or low blood pressure (headaches and fainting spells may give a clue)?   Yes No

12. Do you have difficulty in swallowing (especially important in people who have eating disorders who induce vomiting, causing erosion and fibrosis of the esophagus)?   Yes No

13. Do you have chest pain while swallowing solid food?   Yes No

14. Unexplained numbness in your arms and legs?   Yes No

15. Unexplained and persistent nausea with or
   without vomiting?   Yes No

16. Feeling disconnected from your arms and
   legs? Feeling a loss of sensation from the
   genital area or below the waist?   Yes No

17. Uncontrollable shaking of the hands?   Yes No

18. Unexplained burning, cramping, fullness
   and a "knot" in the stomach?   Yes No

19. Diarrhea because of "nervousness?"   Yes No

20. Have you had periods of bleeding from the
   rectum?   Yes No

21. Have you lost control of your bowel function, especially when you were nervous?   Yes No

22. Have you had periods of rectal pain (unre-
   lated to trauma)?   Yes No

23. Have you had irritable bowel syndrome?   Yes No

24. Have you induced vomiting?   Yes No

25. Have you sustained injuries to your knuckle
   while you tried to get yourself to vomit?   Yes No

26. Have you abused laxatives?   Yes No

27. Have you had pain in your pelvic area?   Yes No

28. Have you had pain in your vagina with or
   without intercourse?   Yes No

29. Have you had problems with pelvic cysts?
   Have you had multiple examinations because of pelvic cysts?   Yes No

30. Have you suffered from endometriosis?   Yes No

31. Have you had severe problems with premenstrual syndrome?   Yes No

32. Do you have scars and mutilation in your
   genital area?   Yes No

33. Have you had a hysterectomy before the
   age of 30?   Yes No

34. Have you had venereal disease? Once? Many
   times?   Yes No

35. Have you had one or more abortions?   Yes   No

36. Have you had pelvic inflammatory disease?   Yes   No

37. Have you had "stress incontinence" or bed-
wetting?   Yes   No

38. Have you had problems of being overweight?   Yes   No

39. Have you had problems of being under-
weight?   Yes   No

40. Do you suffer from chronic fatigue
syndrome?   Yes   No

41. Do you suffer from hypoglycemia?   Yes   No

If you have answered *yes* to many or most of these questions, it means that you may be severely emotionally stressed and are not dealing with it. It may mean that you have memories of childhood that have been blocked and are coming up in the form of physical illnesses. Just like drinking and drugs and other addictions, preoccupation with reacting to and treating the physical illness may be an escape from not dealing with the underlying memories and feelings that often point towards real recovery. Without such work, you may stay sick or even become sicker.

Summary Of Physical Symptoms

In many adult children of dysfunctional families, physical symptoms may be the only clue that suggest they are dealing with repressed emotional pain (shame, rage, guilt, hopelessness). Part of working the 12 Steps, part of taking inventory, part of listening to your inner child's pain is to connect the physical pain and discomfort to stressors in your life, both in the present and in the past. Even if you are only taking nonaddictive medications such as Inderal (for hypertension), Zantac (for stomach ulcers), Motrin (for muscle and joint aches and pains) and Theo-Dur (for shortness of breath and asthma), you are not looking at the cause of these problems, just medicating the effects and, in essence, covering up.

For a co-dependent or an addict in second-stage recovery, medicating themselves and not listening to and working through the physical symptoms of stress is to be in **denial**. Such a person is not working the 12-Step program of recovery.

NINE

Breaking Down Denial

The last three chapters should help you know if your coming from a dysfunctional family environment has something to do with the way you have lived and felt and acted or if your medical problems may be because of the abuse. It should have cracked the walls of denial, even if only a little.

As you attend 12-Step meetings at the same time, denial should begin to break down even further. Recovery can only take place within the structure of a 12-Step program that you organize into your life. It can only happen in an environment where others that share a common pain, a common wounding, can stand up and speak without shame. It cannot happen in a bar. It cannot happen if you choose not to take the time to attend meetings because you are too busy taking care of others.

The walls of denial are incredibly strong. Even after you see the pain of your inner child, you will have a hard time staying connected.

Three months after being in recovery, *Richard* went back to his girlfriend. Soon he was "too busy" trying to mend the relationship.

Even though his girlfriend had been counseled about working on
her co-dependent issues herself, because of her own neediness she
never made an issue of his not attending meetings. He stopped
attending meetings. He felt fine. He remembered the issues in his
head but he "felt good" and thought there was no reason to feel
unhappy. He had not confronted his mother (who had abused and
abandoned him), his sister (who had abused him), his boss (who
had emotionally abused him and put him down and against whom
the patient had tremendous unspoken rage) or his girlfriend.

One month after moving back, he called me up. He had been on
a cocaine binge for the previous nine hours. It had happened after
a fight with his girlfriend.

Denial is an insidious devil. I don't know of any addict or co-
dependent in recovery who sets out saying that they are going to
"slip." It "slips on you" as you move away from working the Steps.

Recovery Is Not Part-Time Work

Recovery: you have to breathe it, sleep it and dream it. You must
want desperately to become better. You must take inventory before
you go to bed and you must take inventory when you wake up. You
must question your dreams and your nightmares. You must ask
yourself why you feel bad when you feel bad and why you feel good
when you feel good. The world is not an easy place for someone for
whom goodness and badness, love and hate, the truth and the lie
have all been distorted. Nothing must be assumed.

Patricia felt good about Christmas. She was going to meet with
her mother. She "forgot" she was also going to be seeing her mother's brother, her uncle who had abused her and molested her many
times and through many years as a child. She had never confronted
him but had just begun to get in touch with the shame, the guilt and
the rage that had caused her to live a depressed, self-abusive, eating-
disordered life, married to an alcoholic. She "forgot" she was going
to meet with her daughter whom she had emotionally and physically
abused and with whom she had not made amends.

After a drunken Christmas party (Patricia did not drink), she felt a
terrible sadness and a terrible anger, and she wished she were dead.
Meeting with her uncle made her feel suicidal. It touched off childhood feelings of guilt (for being "bad" by having sex with her uncle)
and rage towards him and her mother for not protecting her—then
more guilt and self-hate for feeling angry towards her mother.

Meeting with her daughter caused her once again to feel self-hate and question her role as a parent and live with the guilt of her actions. Meeting with her mother brought up tremendous feelings of abandonment and rage that came from her mother's being involved in relationships with alcoholic men who emotionally abused Patricia. She felt rage towards her mother for not protecting her from her uncle who came and abused her whenever he felt like it and about whom the mother did nothing. Patricia had not confronted anyone.

Patricia came to my office wondering why she was feeling lousy. Do you?

The Meaning Of Trauma-Specific Groups

It is important that people attend the meetings that are closest to their own wounding. If you come from an alcoholic home, it is not appropriate for you to attend Alcoholics Anonymous (AA) or Narcotics Anonymous (NA). It is important for you to be in a meeting where others in abusive, alcoholic homes feel free to talk.

If you have a problem with sexual abuse and incest, it is important to go to an Incest Survivors 12-Step meeting. It is not enough, even if that may be the case, to attend only Adult Children of Alcoholics (ACoA) if in fact your incestuous parents were also alcoholics.

If you have a problem with having molested children, it is important that you attend Parents Anonymous (PA). It is also important to attend sexual addiction 12-Step groups. If you have had problems with alcohol or come from an alcoholic home then you must also attend AA and ACoA. It is important to be among people who understand you and, as I said earlier, share a common pain. To not attend meetings that are specific to your trauma is to be in denial. It is to hold back the process of recovery and choose to return to the way of being blind.

People who have incest and sexual abuse issues are not in recovery no matter how many AA, NA, OA, eating disorder or ACoA meetings they attend because they are not looking at feelings and working through their greatest hurt. A person who has battled alcoholism and has been to AA for 20 years may just be a "dry drunk," emotionally out of touch, really not taking inventory and continuing in a passionless lifestyle. This person would need to go to Incest Survivor 12-Step meetings in addition to attending AA and get an incest survivor sponsor, in addition to having an AA sponsor.

Into
The Light

TEN

Healing The Self: Self-Awareness

For most people, the 12 Steps alone are all the therapy that they need to work towards recovery. Sometimes other sources including psychotherapy may help speed it up. *Nothing* will take the place of the 12 Steps.

The reason for not making movement in recovery is usually because of dishonesty on the participant's part. I don't mean dishonesty in a moral way. I mean dishonesty as a process of denial. Going to a church or a school two or three evenings a week to attend AA meetings, eating donuts and drinking coffee does not mean you're working on the 12 Steps.

Do you listen or do you block out what's happening in meetings? Do you ever take chances and open up and talk when you are in meetings? How do you deal with people listening to you? How do you deal with their not listening to you?

It takes more than *acting* like you are in recovery to be in recovery. Recovery group attendance may be good to tell a probation officer about. It may be good enough to please others. It is not good enough for you.

Recovery is a 24-hour, lifelong process that demands **desperation** (desperation as in recovery being *the most important thing in your life*). Consistency, honesty and courage are the key words.

If you are to read the remainder of this book and practice what it says, you will find yourself significantly more connected and stronger in your recovery in six months to a year. The key word is *honesty.*

The Story Of The Priest And The Prostitute

Let me tell you an old joke—a sort of Eastern-Western parable—as an example.

At the crossroads of a little town lived a priest and a prostitute, plying their respective trades across from each other. He, cross-legged and with hands held in the posture of prayer, in his temple, looking with disgust at the goings-on in the house of ill-repute across from him. He heard drunken laughter and seductive words as the woman worked one client after another.

They both get old and die. Comes Judgment Day, and there is St. Peter directing newcomers towards Heaven or Hell, as the case may be. The priest was beside himself with rage when St. Peter directed the prostitute towards Heaven. But when St. Peter directed *him* towards the gates of Hell, he broke down.

"This is not a God that is fair. I prayed all my life, sitting in my temple, avoiding temptations of the flesh, and *I* get to go to Hell while this whore who has sinned all her life gets to go to Heaven? It is not just!"

St. Peter says, "It *is* just, my friend. You may have been praying but your mind was on the whore across the street. She, on the other hand, may have been on her back but her eyes were on the temple and her mind was on God."

ELEVEN

Healing The Body

All the soarings of my mind begin in my blood.

Rainer Maria Rilke

W hy is it that people who are otherwise bright and creative, often very task-oriented, are unable to change the course of their self-destructive, apathetic and angry lives?

Long before you were able to make picture memories, you felt your existence in your body. You felt it in the way that your body was held (or *not* held) by the people who were supposed to love and protect you.

People from a dysfunctional family environment carry the memories of pain, anger, sadness, betrayal, shame and fear in their bodies. They carry the memory of their childhood in their walk, in the way that they stand, how they look at you or don't look at you. Shame makes it hard for a person to stand erect and look people in the eye even when they don't know why they should be ashamed, even when they don't know that they are carrying the shame.

Fear is carried in the muscles of your back and neck. You are like an animal in terror, waiting to spring from some unknown reason, from some unseen enemy that you carry in the recesses of your mind. And you do all this while you walk upright with a smile on your face, like a facade.

Co-dependents and addicts know what it is like not be touched with affection. For them, touch has often been violent or sexualized. They may have never known noncontingent affection and touching.

The healing of the body and the awareness of body memories is an important step in self-awareness as a whole.

Body Work Is Essential For Recovery

Body work can be a major factor in successful therapy:

- For eating disorders (obesity, compulsive over-eating, self-star-vation and forced vomiting).
- For self-mutilation (cutting, burning, slashing, beating on oneself).
- For sexual dysfunction (sexual addiction, promiscuous behavior, inability to enjoy sexual activity, sadomasochistic sexual behavior, pedophilia).
- For problems of rage and violence.
- For severe psychosomatic problems.

My experience is that when people with the above problems do not undergo body work and massage therapy, they will either not recover at all or their progress in recovery will be extremely slow and frustrating.

What Is Body Work?

Without making it sound too complicated, body work is the process of becoming aware of our bodies, recognizing the memories and the feelings of pain, shame, rejection, self-hate and anger that it carries (from having lived in a dysfunctional, abusive and abandoning environment) and using this knowledge for greater degrees of self-awareness. Body work, additionally, helps make our bodies feel the strength and pride and self-love that has to be achieved. It gives us the means to use the body as a vehicle for recovery and growth. Body work consists of:

1. Holding
2. Positioning
3. Body Movement Therapy
4. Body Massage (and relearning the experience of touch in a nonsexualized, nonthreatening manner)

Physical Signs Of Abuse

Following are the physical "signatures" of having had a fearful, uncaring sexualized, shaming and often violently abused childhood. Abused/co-dependent people seem to carry their bodies like they don't belong to them, or they may invest *too much* of themselves in their body in a sexualized or aggressive manner. There is a sense of lack of comfort with their bodies. Either they have to show it off or they're ashamed of it.

The posture of shame. The neck and head are held down, the eyes are downcast or staring away, the face shows no expression or shows a sad expression with lips drooped, the back is bent foward and the shoulders are hunched. Excessive timidity in expression and often inappropriate smiling are part of that sense of shame.

The posture of rage. The eyes are widely open, eyeballs bulging, pupils dilated, nostrils flared and the face is flushed. The chest is often held out in an exaggeration of machismo, a caricature of courage for one who has known great fear coming from the rage of others.

The posture of fear. The posture of fear is one of extreme restlessness or conversely an apathetic lack of movement, as if any movement would cause painful consequences.

The *sexualized* addict/co-dependent may smile too much. Primarily but not exclusively, the female co-dependent and abuse survivor who is sexualized holds and moves the body to accentuate and to show off their breasts and buttocks, the males to show off their genitals. Females often have the "come hither" look in the face and the eyes. An example is Marilyn Monroe whom we now recognize was sexually abused within the multiple foster homes that she grew up in.

Women abuse survivors may also have the opposite body posture and attitude and facial expressions, in which women consciously and unconsciously dowplay their normal sexuality because of the tremendous hidden shame connected to their sexual self. They cannot accept it and feel proud of its being part of themselves. They feel ashamed and deny their sexual self. Women who have been abused may sit, stand and walk in a masculine manner. They make their faces hard, rejecting the innate tenderness of their femininity. Often co-dependent/addict and abuse survivors carry on their faces and bodies a haggard appearance with premature wrinkles and furrows. Those coming from a background of physical abuse often have facial tics suggestive of having lived in a fear-filled environment. It may also suggest that they were slapped around on the face.

Fat is used like many layers of clothing under which a patient hides in a hunched position.

The *movements* — stride, gait — are either sexualized, aggressive, hesitant or jerky, lacking in decisiveness, as if they may have to jump without warning (suggesting deep-seated anxiety and fear) or as if they had nowhere certain to go.

Holding of Babies. A healthy, self-sufficient mother holds her baby with adoration, excitement and respect. She passes on her own sense of inner calm and pride to the child in the way that she walks, coos, holds him close to her when he wants to, gives him room to move when he wants to without feeling rejected herself. Such a child feels safe and yet free, excited without being overwhelmed and has an innate sense of self-esteem.

Anxious, depressed mothers cling to their babies. They cling to the baby when they feel alone and afraid and let go and abandon the child when something or someone else fulfills their own immediate need. Sometimes they will reject the baby if the baby cries too much or doesn't smile back when smiled at.

Angry mothers will distance themselves from the child so as not to hurt or actually abuse the child.

Posture Therapy

Posture therapy involves recognizing and consciously correcting— that is, paying attention to — the way you stand, looking directly at people while talking, holding your shoulders and neck erect. Where a person's movements are very rigid, massage and movement therapy such as dance therapy and Tai Chi can be helpful.

Fear- and shame-molded bodies will show improvement in posture if they work with a massage therapist who, over a period of time, will bring the person to the point where they can stretch out on their backs with their legs extended out straight and have their shoulders, chest, abdomen and flanks massaged. Both light (stroking movement) and deep massage of the muscles should be employed. The massage therapist should establish trust by moving slowly and starting with the hands and feet, and then on to the arms and legs before making any contact with the trunk. Massage can be done through the clothing if the person feels safer that way. If you have a massage therapist, you can let them know that that's the way you would like to start.[1]

Initial reaction to posture-correcting massage therapy, as felt by survivors of sexual and physical abuse, will be to have severe painful spasms of the abdominal muscles and flanks. They may "curl up" in a defensive position by getting on their sides and drawing their knees towards their chest. All work involving body contact has to be done with great respect for the bodily boundaries and should never be rushed. Especially in the beginning, the massage therapist should let the client know where they are going to be touched and how they are going to be moved. If the person is in therapy, the psychotherapist should work closely with the massage therapist.[2]

Chronically depressed, anxious and timid men and women who walk with poor posture, i.e., stooped, hunched shoulders and avoiding eye contact, will be able to reinforce their healthy aggressive self if they wear boots since this compels them to straighten their backs out. I have even found this to be helpful in eventually making them less depressed and in improving their self-esteem.

Women who have problems feeling feminine should experiment with wearing more feminine clothes and high heels. Women who have a sexualized posture would do better getting rid of high heels when they choose to come across in a nonsexualized manner. Abuse survivors, especially from a background of sexual abuse, often do not know that their body is sending out sexual signals. Decreasing these sexual signals by changing and paying attention to bodily postures will help them be taken more seriously and in a nonsexualized manner in situations where that is necessary.

Facial Massage

Spend time exercising the facial muscles, including making frowns and smiles and laughing. Practice screaming loudly if you're a person who is not used to raising your voice even in situations where you need to raise your voice or feel yourself to be excessively intimidated.

Holding Techniques

Being held in a nonthreatening manner helps those with problems of violent behavior, sexualized behavior and sexual addictions. *Initially this may cause great anxiety and even physical pain coming from muscle spasms but being held often releases tremendous amounts of sadness (in those who experience mostly anger and rage and cannot feel sad).* Apathetic and depressed individuals who have missed being held in a protective and affectionate manner, as in the abandonment of a depressed, apathetic, rejecting or intoxicated mother, may experience rage as they feel reconnected to suppressed feelings of their infancy.

After trust has developed between the massage therapist and the client, specialized holding techniques such as being held by the wrists and the ankles, being touched on the back of the head, positioning a person on their knees with their head down and positioning the person on their back and placing pressure on the chest may be helpful in bringing up memories and feelings related to childhood abuse. These may include intense feelings of terror and shame, especially for those who have been sexually or ritualistically abused.

Stroking

Massage and body work must recreate the sensations that were missed or perverted in infancy and childhood. Soft stroking—which in those who have been sexually abused may be responded to with sexual arousal or intense fear with muscle spasms, excessive ticklish feelings and intense anxiety as if they are going to burst—are helpful to desensitize and bring them closer to healthy touching, as well as helping them get in touch with memories and feelings.

Brisk stroking of large muscle groups such as the muscles of the arm (biceps, triceps, deltoids), muscles of the thigh, the back of the thigh and calf are helpful to increase the tone of the muscle and decrease dissociation, especially when they are thinking about painful things and when there is a tendency to depersonalize and "disconnect." These techniques are helpful for reducing anxiety, panic, paranoia and angry agitated feelings, and to help get a person "moving" when they are feeling "down" and cannot use exercise as a way of relieving anxiety.

Deep massage to joints, tendons and muscles for about two weeks will help the person who has not exercised or will encourage one who has stopped exercising to once again begin exercising.

Examples Of Body Work

Tim. Tim developed intense and loud screaming when he was placed on his belly and his arms were raised over his shoulders. He began to experience flashbacks and to relive the feelings and picture memories and bodily motions connected to being beaten and homosexually raped when he was in a juvenile detention facility at the age of 13. He recalled the shame that he had felt at being sodomized by an older adolescent and the anger and homicidal feelings that he felt at the time. Tim's family had always known him to be an extremely rageful person who would fly off the handle with little provocation.

With body work, for the first time in his life, he began to feel a sense of sadness for his inner child and what he had been through, and was able to verbalize anger towards the person who had hurt him. This caused him to have increasingly fewer problems with rage and also many fewer physical problems such as the headaches and colitis he had suffered from throughout his adult life. Working through these feelings and memories in individual therapy and groups, this intelligent and sensitive person, who because of his low self-esteem had always done menial jobs, went on to go to school, becoming a chemical dependency counselor with newfound hope, strength and self-awareness.

Fay. During massage therapy and body work, Fay was positioned on her belly. Being touched on her lower back by the female massage therapist recreated for her the experience of being raped by her father. He would position her on her knees and chest, compel her to take in large amounts of soapy enema water, then rape her both orally and rectally. When she accidentally let go of the water, she would be beaten further and be forced to clean up the mess. Fay is making significant recovery in her long history of alcoholism, eating disorders, dissociation, self-mutilation and suicidal tendencies.

Bob. Bob was hospitalized because he had psychotic hallucinations. While lying on his back during massage work, his chest was touched. He began to have feelings related to being ritualistically tortured. He began to feel suffocated and started screaming and writhing. He began to re-enact a scene in which snakes were placed over his body. After an intense breakdown that lasted for several days during which time intensive psychotherapy, group therapy and holding, both physically and emotionally, was provided for the patient, his paranoid and psychotic symptoms began to decrease and eventually resolve.

Ken. Ken, a middle-aged male homosexual with a history of multiple relapses into cocaine abuse, was held at the wrists and ankles. This caused him to re-experience a rape that had been accomplished by his brother and his brother's friends when he was about eight or nine years old. The patient had been hospitalized because of mood swings, intense agitation and the need to work on second stage recovery from cocaine abuse.

Melodie. Melodie, a 23-year-old incest survivor, extremely promiscuous and sexually addicted, was held for 30 minutes by an older female massage therapist who talked to her gently or just kept quiet during the time that she worked with her, approximately four times a week. Initially she had some difficulty, feeling tense and wanting to push the woman away. But after a period of time, she allowed herself to cry for the first time since she was a very young child. She began to recognize the feelings of abandonment in her childhood when she was never held or given physical affection by her mother. The only physical "affection" that she had received was sexualized by various male members of her family who include her stepfather, her mother's brothers and her stepgrandfather. Working with these feelings and memories in individual therapy and attending 12-Step incest survivor groups, her sexual addictions and mood swings began to decrease and become more manageable.

Art. Art was a schoolteacher with an education on the level of a Master's degree. He had tremendous problems with rage and had been physically violent towards his teenage sons and daughters. While his body was positioned as if he were in a kneeling position and the body work therapist moved her hands on his back, he began to experience a tremendous amount of tears as well as a lot of fear. The trauma of memories of beatings by his father when he was a child was brought out; he had been made to kneel against the bed as his father whipped him on his back.

Who Can Provide Massage?

Ideally, massage and body work should be performed by someone who has had experience with survivors. It is important to do a good background check and obtain references from other patients and therapists before you start with one. In spite of all the recommendations, it is imperative that you maintain boundaries and limits in your massage sessions. If there are things within the session that make you uncomfortable, such as the way you are touched, you need to discuss it with people—including your sponsor and others in your 12-Step meetings, as well as with a therapist if you have one.

The potential for being revictimized, especially sexually revictimized during such physical contact, is present. Becoming excessively emotionally dependent on the massage therapist can become a problem if the therapist does not set boundaries. My advice to women is that they should stay with female massage therapists. My experience is that men respond just as well to male or female massage therapists. Some men may tolerate female massage therapists better than male massage therapists, especially if they have hidden memories of having been violated homosexually.

Self-Massage

Once you have had some basic feeling of comfort in your body from therapeutic massage, you should use this as a way to learn how to massage yourself and to recreate the same feelings, especially those of comforting (self-soothing). Self-massage is unlikely to create flashbacks or make you more anxious. Massage your forehead, the back of your head, your neck, shoulders, arms, hands, thighs calves and feet. Do this about three times a day, spending at least ten minutes doing so. Stretching and yawning both in the beginning and the end of such a massage can be both invigorating and relaxing.

Autonomic Massage

By this I mean a brisk shower, alternating between very hot (but not scalding) and very cold water, three to five minutes each time, for approximately 15-20 minutes while briskly massaging your body either with your hands or with a washcloth. I have found this method very helpful when patients have called me up complaining of overwhelming anxiety/panic reactions, depersonalization (feeling numb, unreal and disconnected from the body in response to overwhelming emotional pain) and for the severe fatigue of depression when the arms and legs feel like they weigh a ton, even when doing the laundry, making a cup of tea or getting up from bed seems like an impossible task. Such hot/cold sensations stimulate your autonomic nervous system and help fight anxiety. This kind of shower can get you up and about so you can go on to your 12-Step meetings and all the other steps that you need to take towards recovery.

Self-massage is going to be helpful only if it is done on a regular basis. Unlike massage from someone else, it does not cost you any money, so you have no excuses. If it is not done regularly, you will not feel like doing it when you need to.

Summary

Massage and body work are an invaluable treatment for depression with severe apathy, eating disorders, self-mutilation, violent behavior, rage problems, sexual addictions and for perverse sexual behavior among both men and women.

I have found massage therapy especially useful in treating frigidity, hypersexuality, severe premenstrual syndrome, and pain related to endometriosis and pelvic cysts in women. It has also been helpful in migraine, asthma and irritable bowel syndrome. Massage is an important and often vital element in recovery from violent physical abuse as well as sexual and ritual abuse. It cuts the treatment time towards recovery significantly. It allows a person to be able to do without using medications such as Xanax and Valium.

Massage And Self-Awareness

Massage brings back the feelings and picture-memories connected with abuse and elicits flashbacks, allowing for increased self-awareness.

It promotes a sense of bodily boundaries which have been damaged by physical, mental and sexual abuse. It also begins to help the patient connect to feelings of self-soothing so that they can then embark on a course in which they can stroke themselves *for* themselves, as opposed to being stroked by somebody else or not being stroked at all.

It helps people with sexualized and violent childhoods experience a touching that is neither sexualized or violent. It decreases anxiety which feels like a cringing of the skin among some people. This is easy to see when the thoughts of being touched are associated with being hurt or being sexually abused, or for a person who has been so neglected in touching as an experience in life that it feels unfamiliar and frightening.

Being touched, held and massaged by another human being in a noncontingent fashion is the cornerstone to recovery, especially from preverbal wounds. Without such therapy, the disorders that I have discussed earlier may not fully recover or may take a very long time to recover.

I will say, at the cost of creating a controversy, that for many addicts and co-dependents who are blocked in recovery or relapse often because of bodily memories of emotional pain, *not to have massage and body work is not to work towards recovery.* As long as they dread being touched or having their bodies held by another human being, they live with a certain sense of fear, shame and self-hate and are not working through it.

The time has come for you to love your body, to hold it as it has never been held, with love, with care and with pride. The sooner the abuse survivor, co-dependent and addict in second-stage recovery comes to that point, the further they will be on the road to recovery.

I also encourage abuse survivors to get nonsexual massage and holding from significant others in their life on a regular basis. Massage acts as a "chemical window," in that changes in brain and body chemicals take place while the person is being massaged. This creates a state of mind and body in which previous experiences of harmful touching can be changed.

Without feeling loved or loving oneself, we are blind, we are deaf. To be touched and held unconditionally can give a sense of being loved, respected and cared for as no words can. A sense of caring, not being taken for granted and being given attention are all better absorbed and understood while a person is being massaged. It must, therefore, form an essential part in the work of recovery for abuse survivors.

Massage Helps Treat Dissociation

For people who tend to dissociate, massage in the beginning can often increase that tendency. Over a period of time, however, getting a massage from someone and learning to self-massage will help people keep more in touch with themselves and with what it going on around them by becoming more aware and relaxed.

I often tell people to tape-record sessions that they are having with their therapists or under hypnosis, especially memories related to physical, mental and sexual abuse. When they listen to their tapes, they begin to dissociate as emotionally painful material begins to be heard. Once again, massage can help to hear things fully and not "space out" and to keep people in touch with their feelings, be it feelings of anger, sadness, rage or fear.

Massage therapy is extremely helpful in the treatment of dissociative disorders which are universally common in people who come from a background of abuse. While the classic example is multiple personality disorder, my observation and the experiences of others indicate that *almost everyone who goes through a traumatic childhood with unhealed wounds tends to dissociate;* that is, to live in their heads and disconnect from their bodies. It is like being dead even when one knows that one is alive. It is this agonizing sense of deadness that often drives a person back into drugs, destructive habits and relationships.

Massage brings to the life of such people the fullness of experience. It allows them to fully recognize their aliveness, to feel completely with their bodies and their minds and to feel like a complete person.

---

1. I have known people, mainly women, but also some men, who have gone to people for massage and were told by the massage therapist on the first meeting that they need to take their clothes off, and in a robot-like manner did so, and then felt that they were terribly violated. A good massage therapist who has worked with abuse survivors will not do this. However, once again, abuse survivors themselves have to make sure that they are not mistreated and need to bear this in mind when they undertake massage therapy.

2. I generally suggest that the psychotherapist not be physically present, even when the patient is of the same sex, because of the concern of blurring roles. However, flashbacks and any kind of disturbances noticed during the massage therapy session should be passed on to the psychotherapist so he or she can work in therapy with the client. It may help to tape the session, where the person expresses the feelings and thoughts brought about during body work.

TWELVE

Role Of Exercise In Recovery

While the positive role of exercise cannot be covered in a single chapter, my emphasis here is that *all* abuse survivors, co-dependents and addicts need to exercise in a healthy manner.[1]

To broadly summarize the role of exercise in mind-body healing, we can note eight major benefits:

1. Daily exercise improves the quality of sleep. Insomnia, excessive sleep and poor quality of sleep are universally present in the survivor, co-dependent and addict population. Poor quality sleep can often be a clue to having grown up in a dysfunctional family environment.

2. Exercise improves the tone of the muscles. Over a period of time, exercise helps to correct unhealthy postures brought about by a lifetime of shame, self-hate, lack of pride, lack of self-esteem and fear.

3. Exercise decreases the physical symptoms of anxiety. Abuse survivors, co-dependents and addicts have a dysautonomic

condition, namely that their autonomic nervous system is unstable. Such persons, instead of feeling and knowing why they feel anxious, go on to only feel the bodily symptoms of anxiety such as light-headedness, palpitations of the heart, shakiness and trembling of the arms and legs, out-of-control breathing and shortness of breath, uneasy feelings in the gut, an urgency to go to the bathroom when they get nervous and hot and cold sensations, especially in their arms and legs, when they are upset.

4. Exercise strengthens the working of the autonomic nervous system. Instead of feeling only discomfort through their body, they begin to feel and think about what is bothering them; this gets them closer towards increasing awareness of their feelings and thoughts and therefore towards recovery.
5. Exercise makes you physically healthier. Exercise improves the immune system.[2]
6. By changing brain chemicals, exercise often contributes towards recovery in depression.
7. Exercise helps control weight gain.
8. Exercise can help self-soothing, relaxation and provide a "safe space" during overwhelming emotional crisis.

In the abuse survivor, exercise has a much greater significance. *Addicts often act impulsively, reactively, explosively or compulsively. Co-dependents have a persistent failure to act and have a problem with apathy or compulsivity.* They will stay on in jobs, marriages and relationships without acting to change. They allow themselves to be abused in an apathetic manner. It is this apathy, this passivity, that prevents them from making decisive changes in their lives from taking charge. Exercise on a regular basis will help to change these characteristics.

If, from the very beginning of your life, you have felt that your body and your mind do not belong to you—having lived through the reality of being physically and sexually abused, your most private spaces assaulted, your body tortured—you have learned to disown your body. You have learned to do nothing and lie still because to do something brings more punishment.

You bottle up your feelings until you explode in rage or in self-destructive behavior.

Visualize the muscles of your body like the cutting edge of your will. Your muscles are where your mind makes your body move—move to take action or not to act.

Exercise strengthens the cables between the mind and the body and takes you from apathetic, compulsive and impulsive actions to decisive adult actions. It helps you regain power. It tells you, in a very real way, that you are in control.

It tells you at a nonverbal level, more than any therapist can teach you, that you can make changes. That you can leave an abusive spouse or boyfriend, obtain a restraining order, change a job, move away from destructive "friends," destructive environments, stop someone from hurting you, push someone away from making unwanted advances on your body, or walk away.

It tells you that you can scream, that you can protect yourself. It tells you that you are in charge of your body and therefore in charge of your actions, good or bad, and that you make the choices.

People who exercise feel emotionally more courageous. They can overcome the barrier of fear and shame that prevents them from thinking about shameful and fearful things in their lives—both in the present and in the past.

It allows them to make a fearless journey into the grief, rage, shame and guilt of childhood. It allows them to begin to start looking people in the eye.

Exercise is the perfect time for taking inventory.

During exercise, **Mike,** an alcoholic, was encouraged to recall how he molested his four-year-old stepson. Because of his denial, fear and shame whenever he thought about this, he would block it out. During exercise, he began to have increasing picture-memories of how he molested his stepson. He also began to recall, for the first time, his own molestation in childhood by his father and his grandfather. He had completely blocked all of this out, and it was in fact the cause of his own sexual addiction and pedophilic tendencies. Awareness of the roots of his own compulsive sexual addiction began to help him towards his recovery with a much greater degree of honesty.

Sharon would go into a childlike fright with intense terror when she talked about her father's violent sexual assault. She would hide behind a chair or flee into a corner and curl up into a ball. She would sometimes lose control of her bladder as these feelings of intense terror would overwhelm her.

I had her tape these sessions of disclosures and had her listen to them while she exercised on a stationary bike. Instead of dissociating or regressing (curling up into a ball like a frightened child), she began to experience appropriate anger, anger that she previously had not felt towards her father since she had never dealt with fully remembering at a feeling and thinking level of how viciously he had abused her.

This began to help the patient resolve some of the intense self-hate, low self-esteem and depression that had caused her to have severe eating disorders, withdrawal, sexual problems and co-dependency that had plagued her throughout her late teens and her entire adult life.

Exercise: How Often And What Kind

Exercise must be daily or at least five times a week. Preferably, it should be in the early part of the day. Since procrastination is a major problem with survivors, addicts and co-dependents, it is best to get done with exercise early in the day. It prepares you to face the rest of the day better.

Exercise should be done for at least a half hour and should be enough to cause you to feel your heart pound and cause you to sweat. It should leave you, at least momentarily, short of breath during the course of every session. It should cause you to have some amount of tension and twitching in your muscles, at least for a brief time, after you are done with it. The idea is that it should stimulate your autonomic nervous system.

This exercise is something that should be done alone. It is easy to feel motivated when you have friends and you have been presented with a new jogging suit or you have just lost 20 pounds and are willing to show off your body. However, exercise is most important on those days when it feels like the whole world has deserted you and you are full of shame, self-hate and a paralysis of the will. These are the days that you must get out of bed, stand up straight and begin the process of working out, begin to wash out some of that shame that does not belong to you.

However, unless it is done by habit, unless it becomes entrenched as something that comes into your day on a daily basis, like clockwork, it is unlikely that you will be able to exercise during times when you really need to do it.

Walking, while being a relaxing habit, will not cause the kind of stimulation of the autonomic nervous system or release the endorphines that come from heavy exercise like running, aerobics or skipping rope.

Aerobic exercises are best, i.e., running, a Jane Fonda-type of workout, running up and down the stairs, or playing basketball. For some, in addition to aerobic exercises, isometric exercises such as lifting weights may be helpful. Generally speaking, however, lifting weights is not recommended.

Aggressive exercises that couple coordination and mental concentration (like karate), that involve kicking, decisive and powerful thrusts of the extremities, screaming aggressive sounds and making lunges are helpful for victims of incest and sexual abuse. *Overcoming the bodily sense of being a victim,* being restrained, restricted and paralyzed by fear through the childhood years will help them get in touch with the healthy, aggressive feelings. Such exercises will also tap into hidden anger.

Exercise increases coordination. For people who feel out of control and unbalanced, coordinating exercises will bring a sense of "balance" if done on a regular basis.

Exercise is important for abuse survivors, co-dependents and addicts. For obese, frightened, anxious women who have many physical complaints that seem to know no cures and cannot experience anger; who have sexual problems and eating disorders, who cannot enjoy their bodies in sports, sex or play, exercise is *absolutely necessary. Without exercise, they really cannot be in recovery. No matter what other efforts they make towards recovery, if it is not augmented with exercise, they will never be able to begin to experience a real sense of power at a subconscious level. This will hinder any kind of progress in recovery.*

I have often seen people make tremendous strides, including increasing their self-esteem, making life changes and also starting to attend 12-Step meetings with greater ease once they start exercising on their own.

Exercise begins to change a person's false sense of control or overcontrol and bring about a sense of true control that comes from within. But again, I emphasize that exercise has to be done by habit, on a daily or least a five-times-a-week basis for it to work, to help you towards recovery, to fight depression, decrease obesity problems, increase self-esteem and increase self-awareness.

A Mental Exercise: The Relaxation Response

For increasing self-awareness and self-soothing, there is a condition of body and mind you can create anytime and anywhere.

In a 20-year study at Harvard's New England Deaconess Hospital (Mind-Body Institute), Dr. Herbert Benson and his colleagues have shown that 20 minutes of using the technique that he calls the relaxation response can significantly help people with problems such as chronic pain, hypertension, premenstrual syndrome and sleep disturbances. There is evidence that changes in lifestyle involving such exercises may help with outcomes of cancer and even AIDS.

The relaxation response essentially consists of providing yourself a safe place for about a half hour every day, twice a day, morning and evening, with repeating a word in a prayer-like manner. You can use any word that you feel comfortable with, including your name.[3]

Attention is paid to breathing. Take deep breaths all the way into your stomach (but not to the point of passing out). This rhythmic breathing and repetition of words allows you to detach yourself from your surroundings and begin an inward journey. For those who become very anxious with sitting still, this exercise and repetition of words in a prayer-like manner for 20 minutes can be done while exercising, such as using an exercise bicycle, rowing machine or running. It can be reinforced by listening to soothing music, hearing a tape that presents soothing sounds such as the waves of the ocean, sounds of the forest, etcetera.

The practice of the relaxation response is not connected to any religious dogma and is completely consistent with practicing the 12 Steps.

---

1. That is, not in an addicted or excessive manner where exercise is seen as a way of running away from problems or putting too much importance into looking good as opposed to feeling good; or where exercise is used to compulsively lose weight as in some anorexics.

2. Exercise, by stimulating the autonomic nervous system, may have a positive effect on the immune system into which the autonomic nervous system is "hard wired." Strenuous exercise releases growth hormone which helps the growth of muscle tissue, blood cells, thymus gland and other tissues. The thymus gland regulates the immune system. Exercise, by stimulating the growth hormone, helps to regulate sleep patterns. Exercise releases endorphines which may promote a state of mental well-being. Endorphines may also have a positive effect on the immune system.

Immune system disorders include allergies, psoriasis, asthma, lupus and colitis. Excessive proneness to viral infections and chronic fatigue syndrome may all be helped by regular exercise.

3. Benson, Herbert, M.D., **The Relaxation Response**. New York: William Morrow and Company, Inc., 1975; Benson, Herbert, M.D., with Proctor, William, **Beyond the Relaxation Response—How to Harness the Healing Power of Your Personal Beliefs**. Los Angeles: Times Books, 1984.

THIRTEEN

Healing The Mind With Memory Work

Those who do not remember the past are compelled to repeat it.

George Santayana

People (patients and others) ask me very often if it is important to remember the abuse—and the details of the abuse—in situations having to deal with growing up in a dysfunctional, abandoning, shame-inducing, rage-producing, often violent, alcoholic household.

My answer, which angers many survivors, is *yes.* **It is absolutely important to remember your past if you want to understand and correct the present and move on to the future.**

Compared to the depth of abuse in dysfunctional families—that people have lived through at the hands of their parents, step-parents, grandparents, uncles, aunts, family "friends," older siblings, cousins—the word "abuse" seems like an understatement.

For example, there is *Joanne*. "I was six years old. It was a Saturday morning. My mother told me that me and my brother Tony [age four] would spend the weekend with Bob [mother's boyfriend of the last two months] because she had to go to work. We went to his apartment. He didn't talk much while he drove. He said we were going to have a good time. There wasn't much in his apartment. No toys. My brother and I stayed close in the kitchen, sort of holding onto each other. We were shaking. I began to get scared. Bob didn't talk to us but I heard him making phone calls in the other room. He was up and laughing. He made phone call after phone call. I thought he was calling up people to come over. I thought there was going to be a party but I was getting more scared. My tummy didn't feel good.

"The first person who came was a security guard. We saw him come into the other room. He was dressed like a policeman. He had a gun. Soon, others came. They talked loudly, sometimes softly and then laughed loudly. They seemed to be drunk. Many of them brought beer and other kinds of booze with them. Sometimes they looked in Tony's and my direction and said things to one another. We were beginning to feel real scared.

"Bob called me and Tony into the other room. He said we were going to have a little fun. They had pulled the blinds and bolted the door. My legs were shaking. Everyone was looking at me. Bob told me to take my clothes off. He said it was okay, just do it. The security guard moved, grabbed Tony by his neck, pulled out his gun and stuck it to his head. Bob said, 'Your brother's going to be killed, and it will be your fault if you don't take off your clothes.' I was sobbing and choking. I felt a scream building inside but I didn't hear any sounds. I peed on myself and I was ashamed.

They were pulling the clothes off Tony. He was crying. They punched him, they slapped him. 'Shut the fuck up.' They began pulling at his clothes. Then they had him take all his clothes, including his shorts, off. He bent and tried to cover his genitals with his hand and they laughed. They tied him to the front of the kitchen table legs. They taped his mouth. He kept looking at me. He didn't fight. I could see from his eyes that he was scared. They marched me into the other room. I turned around, I could see my brother looking at me. They pulled the mattress off the metal cot in the living room. They had me take off all my clothes. I felt weak. Bob took me by the hand and led me to the bed. I was feeling very cold and I was shaking.

"The security guard pulled my hands above my head, put the handcuffs on one wrist, then moved the handcuffs over the head end frame of the bed, and put the cuffs on the other wrist. Bob kept telling that I was going to like it. He called me 'cunt,' 'whore.'

"He told me that he had seen me looking at him. (I had looked inside my mother's bedroom a few weeks ago when she had gone to work and Bob was propped up and his legs were spread and he had his hands around his penis and he was reading a magazine. I kept on looking at his penis and I looked up and he was looking at me. I had felt funny, kind of scared, kind of ashamed but I quickly turned around and left. I didn't tell Mommy about it. I knew that she and Bobby were friends. I didn't think she would believe me. They used to drink and laugh loudly together and I didn't think that she would believe me over him. I thought I had been bad.)

"They pulled me down on the bed until my shoulders hurt, they pulled my legs apart and tied my ankles to the rail at the foot of the bed. "I could not move. They made jokes about my "pussy." Bobby said Tony would die if anyone found out. He said my mother would not believe me because I was a lying bitch. He said that they would have to kill Mommy if I told her. I kept praying to God. I wished my mommy would come. The security guard was the first. He pulled down his pants, pulled out his penis and kept rubbing it all the time, looking at me. He put his gun beside my head, on the bed. He kissed me and tried to put his tongue in my mouth. He smelled of beer. He tried to get his penis inside but it hurt, and I kept trying to pull my legs together.

"I began to sob and then scream, and he slapped me many times. Someone put their hands on my mouth, others held my chest down, people held my legs tight so I couldn't squirm. The security guard tried again. I felt I was being torn apart. I felt like throwing up. I felt I was suffocating with the hand over my mouth. I thought I was going to be killed. I think I fainted. Everything became blurry.

"When I awoke, he kept moving his body in and out, and I felt like I was being crushed. I could see other men around the bed, not the faces, just masturbating as they watched. The security guard made grunting and gasping sounds. He then climbed on top of my face and put his penis inside my mouth. Someone else climbed between my legs and put their thing inside me. I felt gagged and choking, like I was going to throw up. I felt the sheet to be wet under my buttocks as I moved. Someone grabbed my hair to hold my head still. I fainted again.

"I woke up, never fully after that. I was limp. One after another. They came and put their penises inside me, masturbated and came over my face and chest, and rubbed their things on me. Someone put his fingers inside my backside, and then his penis. I felt pain. I was sweating. My body kept on moving but I felt limp. I felt I was just watching, like I was outside my body. All the others were breaking and sitting on the floor, leaning back against the wall and drinking while others would come and rape me. I don't know when it became dark.

"I know at some time they were doing things to Tony in the other room. I could hear sounds and laughter. I could hear Tony make sounds through his nose. I felt sad for my brother. I wished I could take the gun and kill them.

"It became the next day. They were mostly gone. Some of them came to me and told me that they knew I had liked it. The security guard was the last to be gone. He took off the handcuffs. He kept winking and leering at me. My ankles were untied. Bobby was picking up the bottles on the floor and putting them in a black trash bag. He came over and sat beside me. I still had no clothes on. He talked to me real nice. He asked if I was hurting (I could not move). My shoulders were raw. My hips were raw, and down there was like burning and raw. He lifted me and carried me to the other room.

"Tony was on the floor, not looking, his knees drawn up towards his chest, his arms around his knees, head down. Sometimes his shoulders would come up like he was sobbing. Bobby brought me my clothes and told me to wait while he got us something to eat. We clung to each other, my brother and I, on that cold floor, without saying anything. Bobby came in with cheeseburgers, fries and Cokes and a couple of bags of M&Ms. I didn't feel like eating, even though he kept telling me to eat. Tony began to eat without saying anything. Bobby kept saying, 'Remember, this is our secret. Don't tell your mother.'

"This went on for months after Bobby moved in. He would treat me special when he was at home like I was his girlfriend. Sometimes Tony and him and me would all get into bed together. Mommy caught Bobby and me in bed. She threw him out and beat me until I was black and blue. She said I was a whore.

"My teacher at school saw the bruises and took me to the nurse. They kept me there in the nurse's office. They asked me about Mommy, about Bobby, about Tony. Soon, there were lots of grown-ups in the office. I didn't go back home that day. They took Tony and me to a foster home. I was scared that I wouldn't see Mommy.

She came and saw me and Tony after two days. She was crying. Later, a few days, we went back home. My mother stopped working for a while. I went to court and a lot of people talked to me. I was frightened. They asked about Bobby. I didn't want my mommy to be hurt or killed. I didn't want anything to happen to Tony."

Joanne's mother's boyfriend shot himself before he was arraigned. Joanne felt guilty about the death of her mother's boyfriend. She thought it was her fault.

I saw her when she was 18. She was an anorexic-looking, hyperactive child-woman who laughed and joked a lot. She became withdrawn when questioned about her childhood. She had been hospitalized after having overdosed following a fight with her current boyfriend. She had a year-old daughter who she loved. She had one previous overdose for which she had been hospitalized and two hospitalizations for chemical dependency, for taking everything including cocaine, heroin, alcohol and LSD. She had problems with promiscuous behavior. She latched onto violent, abusive relationships. She was always drawn towards abusive, substance-abusing older men. Her daughter's father, who was not an alcoholic or chemically dependent man and who didn't physically abuse her, was a year older than she. He separated from her after their brief affair because she become verbally abusive to him, hit him, went out with other men and flashed this in his face. She also refused to give up drugs.

Her hospitalization under my care followed the overdose because her child's father attempted through the courts to gain full custody of the child. The patient was living with her mother at the time. Through psychotherapy, hypnosis, dream work and later on through the use of massage and body work techniques, the extensive history of physical, mental and sexual abuse described by the patient earlier came to be known and worked through in therapy, both in the hospital and upon leaving the hospital. She was initiated into attending 12-Step Alcoholics Anonymous (AA) meetings as well as Incest Survivors 12-Step meetings.

Extremely bright (I.Q. of 140) and vivacious, sometimes child-like, sometimes old beyond her years, Joanne had previously been sexually abused by her maternal grandfather (who also abused her mother) between the age of two and four. After her mother's boyfriend abused her sexually when she was about six years old, her natural father abused her when she was 12. She reported the abuse of her natural father and he was jailed for six months. She said the hardest thing was facing him in court.

I met with her natural father when she was hospitalized. He was a recovered alcoholic, had found religion and described the incident as "one time" when he was tired and intoxicated and lay beside his daughter, his genitals to her back while she was sleeping. He said he was confused. He thought it was his wife (the patient's stepmother). The patient stated that she had had genital sexual intercourse with her father, after he woke her up one night from sleep. It was at a time when she had left her mother's home because of fights with her mother and had been briefly living with her father. When Joanne was asked why she had not fought off her father, the patient replied that she felt paralyzed when she was touched sexually. "My body acted on its own. I was frozen. I was numb."

Joanne is putting the pieces of her life together. She is increasingly connected to the sadness, the sense of betrayal and rage of her childhood. She is working through her guilt. She feels like she is on the edge a lot. She sleeps poorly and wakes up screaming and sweating with nightmares. She has problems with eating disorders. She has long periods of self-starvation with periods of binging. She has not been drinking or using drugs for sometime. She attends Narcotics Anonymous (NA) and Incest Survivors Anonymous (ISA) 12-Step meetings regularly. She has been in a year-long relationship with a non-abusive man, three years older than she. She has mood swings and storms of rage "for no apparent reason" at her husband. She cannot function with him sexually or "just gives in," lying there until he is done. She has fantasies of orgiastic sex with intense feelings of guilt over such fantasies. However, with 12-Step meetings and a sponsor and some continuing psychotherapy, she works at staying connected to where it all came from. She feels hope. She has excellent SAT scores and a scholarship to go on to one of the University of California institutions. She wants to be a psychologist. And she has *not* abused her child.

What Memories Are Made Of

In the early 1950s, Wilder Penfield, a Canadian neurosurgeon working at the Montreal Neurologic Institute, electrically stimulated the brain of a person who was having brain surgery. The patient recalled, in fact relived, intense moments of a forgotten childhood. She could smell the cooking in her mother's kitchen.

For some of us, there are memories of benevolent and caring parents and grandparents, cheerful Christmases and holidays. For others who have been abused and traumatized, it is less pleasant but the brain forgets nothing.

Memory consists of many things but most important of all are the feeling memories. At a very early age, long before you could put together the things that you saw, you retained "picture memories"— things that you heard, felt and smelled. You experience things in your body, in your gut. Even when a child becomes capable of making picture memories, it still "feels" in the gut and in the body much more intensely than what he or she remembers by "picture memories."

Getting in touch with memories involves getting in touch with feelings, gut feelings, skin sensations, sights, sounds and smells. It means getting in touch with the feelings of a frightened little child inside you, who held its body with shame and fear in the closet or under the covers with its hands covering its ears so it was not possible to hear Father beating up Mother and Mother's screams.

Bodily feelings are the feelings of lonely terror from a child's trembling body, the pounding of its heart, the sickening sensation in its stomach, and a feeling that it is going to lose control of bladder and bowels.

Time after time, I have talked with people who can tell you in great detail about things that happened to them—cruel, painful, agonizing incidents. They will talk about them without feeling— often with a smile, without expression or in a nonchalant manner as if they were describing a movie or someone else's story.

It is common for people who have had a painful childhood to remember the events but disconnect the feelings. Memory work in this instance is connecting to the feelings. Those memories are the ones that are in place before a child is even three or four years old and these are what color its life, determining how in life will be acted out. From then on, the feelings become stronger or weaker. It is the original pain at an early age that is hardest to get to and hardest to heal.

There are many ways to get in touch with memories of childhood. It is the process of getting to know, to understand your inner child, its pain, agony and tears, its screams and sorrows, and most of all, its strength and courage—because it has survived.

Memory Work Steps

1. Taking The Time

Taking the time to think with a clear head is important. Without this step no other steps are possible. You have to take the time to think about your past, your childhood, where you came from. If you are in an alcoholic or drug fog, you cannot think. If you are in the grip of an addictive relationship, if you are hurrying from pleasing one person to another, if you are in the throes of self-pity as you continuously allow yourself to be abused, you cannot even begin to think.

For co-dependents, this means taking the time away from those that they are enmeshed with. For addicts, it means becoming sober. It means taking the time to attend meetings.

Just keep in mind that what you will begin to remember is mostly what you had wished to forget when you were a child.

2. Stopping Chemical Addictions

It is absolutely essential to stay away from drugs and alcohol if one is to do memory work. Drugs and alcohol prevent the cognitive work, i.e., the work of thinking through. They cause an organic brain disorder; that is, it affects the brain in such a way that the person's capacity to hear and process things, read and process things, remember and process things and make connnections are all affected.

Jim, an active alcoholic, went through absolute depression and hopelessness with suicidal feelings when his employer of 16 years moved to Arizona and told Jim that although he was a valued employee and they would compensate him, they could not accommodate him in their newer but smaller operation in Arizona. On the surface, it was hard to imagine why a grown man should be driven to suicide from being dropped from a company. He was a skilled technician and had received multiple job offers in the last several years. He could have obtained work elsewhere.

I had him attend AA meetings and started seeing him in therapy. Over a period of time, it became clearer that Jim had an idealized relationship with his employer who in a way had become the father he never had. Jim's entire life in the last 16 years revolved around work and pleasing his employer. More details emerged. He and his mother had been abandoned by his alcoholic, biologic father while he was still an infant. His mother quickly remarried to a man whom Jim, eager for affection, had quickly latched onto and had become very close to. Jim adored his stepfather.

When Jim was 14, his stepfather left abruptly because of problems with Jim's mother. Even though his stepfather told Jim that it was not his fault, Jim felt a terrible abandonment, became depressed and rageful with overt, self-destructive and suicidal behaviors at this time. He began to steal. He began to drink heavily. He pushed his wounds away from consciousness with his alcoholism.

The current rejection from his previously adored supervisor triggered off memories and feelings of the rejection, both at the age of 14 and intense abandonment in his infancy when his biologic father left him. He had suppressed and denied these feelings. Jim had to get out of the alcoholic fog, to stop drinking and to start making the connections to work his way out of that terrible depression.

3. Attending Trauma-Specific Groups

If you are not attending groups that are specific to your kind of wounding, then you are not in recovery. It is important, as I have said in earlier chapters, to attend groups with people who had the same problems in childhood that you did.

Incest survivors who come from alcoholic families and who also have cocaine problems are not going to remember things related to the incest trauma if all they do is attend CA or NA groups or even ACA meetings. Such people need, in addition, to be in a group where the members' hurts are closest to what they have been through. *The mental pictures created by listening to people who have gone through a similar experience of being hurt will unlock the memories and feelings in the person who is listening to them.* Dissociation is possible, therefore it is important to pay attention in these groups. It may help to massage your body and self-soothe while you are in these meetings so you can continue to attend and not "space out" or become overwhelmed with anxiety.

The Vietnam veteran may be seen as being repulsive, shocking and insensitive when he talks, seemingly without feelings about how he was injured by the body parts of his buddy who stepped on a land mine—even if the listener is a rape or incest survivor. Only another Vietnam veteran who has been through what he has been through can fully relate to the agony of being in the dehumanizing environment of war and come up with the feelings and memories of a similar kind that would allow him to empathize with such a person.

Therefore, incest survivors need to attend incest and sexual abuse 12-Step meetings, ACAs need to attend ACA meetings and sexual addicts have to attend sexual addiction meetings. They have to get a sponsor from these groups. When they hear another person talk about the shame, fear and pain of being driven to a compulsion—describing specific acts and incidents—it begins to break down the walls of denial, forgetfulness and repression in listeners, and they start remembering and feeling—an important step in working through to recovery.

Juanita, a 30-year-old school teacher, is an alcoholic and self-mutilator. She has had a history of eating problems and chronic sleep disturbances. She had been attending AA meetings for three years after having moved from the East Coast to the Los Angeles area. She continued through this time to feel depressed and suicidal, to self-mutilate and occasionally to drink. Her knuckles were bruised, infected and swollen from repeatedly hitting the wall. She didn't talk in AA groups. No one in the AA group talked about self-mutilation. She felt that they thought that she was weird. She thought that they could not relate to her.

Upon consulting with me, I told her to start attending ISA meetings as a necessary part of her program and to continue attending AA meetings to maintain her sobriety. She eventually got a sponsor who herself was an incest survivor.

In the first ISA meeting she heard "nothing"—she blocked out everything. The fourth time she attended the meeting, she heard another group member talk about how her father would have her masturbate him (massage his penis) when she was a child so he could "fall asleep." Juanita began to shake and sweat. She felt nauseous. She could feel a scream building up inside her. She felt suicidal. A flood of memories of incestuous abuse by her father who did almost exactly the same thing came up. Juanita went into a crisis from being flooded by such memories but she also connected more and more and she began to understand where her guilt, self-hate and the need for addictive self-mutilation came from.

By attending ISA meetings, by the careful use of hypnosis and at some point, body work and massage, the patient became fully aware of the degree of abuse that had taken place. It began to make sense to her why she had been hospitalized when she was 14 or 15 for a severe eating disorder and how none of this had been spoken about at that time.

I talked with her sisters. They had also been abused. After some initial hesitation, they opened up to her. She was supported by them. Together they confronted their father. While the father denied everything, it became very clear to this patient that she needed to work through some of her rage towards him and get beyond it. She had no connection with her father from that time on. She has a certain degree of sadness about it but she is able to live through the day. She has written letters of confrontation to him. She is less destructive to herself now. She has remained sober and continues to work through a 12-Step program and attend AA and ISA meetings.

This is definitely one instance where memory work made all the difference in this patient's recovery.

John, a Vietnam veteran and alcoholic, with a history of episodic violent behavior and suicide attempts: "When I went to AA meetings, I came out feeling terrible. I didn't think anyone would understand a baby killer and a rapist. I didn't feel I could talk about it. I felt that they would hate me.

"I went to an AA meeting for Vietnam veterans. The first time this guy was talking about how he got hurt in Vietnam, how he was knocked unconscious and hit in the head and shoulder by body parts of a buddy who had stepped on a land mine. He said this without feeling. Something in my gut told me he knew—knew where *I* was coming from. I knew he had been there, been where no 19-year-old should ever have to go.

"I walked up to him and held him, and he held me. We cried and sobbed. We held each other tightly. We said nothing. The group was very supportive. I felt I did more work in my recovery that one evening than I had in attending other AA meetings in the last 14 years."

Honesty is the key. A classic example of people who *think* that they are working in recovery while not doing so are people who attend Weight Watchers and Eating Disorder 12-Step meetings, but who refuse to attend Incest and Sexual Abuse 12-Step meetings "because it is too painful." It is much easier to describe in a roomful of other fat women your struggles and triumphs over a box of donuts than to think, feel, talk or hear about the absolute gut-wrenching, nausea-producing experience of being raped and sodomized in the stark loneliness and terror of your own parents' home—when any semblance of love for your body and healthy sexuality was shattered, seemingly forever, to be replaced by an addiction for food.

4. Journaling

This is a way of recovering memories, taking inventory and getting in touch with your inner child by putting on paper, on a daily basis, your unspoken or spoken, very private thoughts and feelings both from the present and from the past. *Absolute honesty is the key.* You also have to do it consistently or else you are only going to do it during times of crisis or when you feel good and "motivated." Set aside 20 minutes every night, at least five times a week, Monday through Friday, to do it. Make it a habit. If you should feel uncomfortable, if you feel like skipping, the trick is to do it anyway, especially when you are unmotivated. That can happen only by habit and daily effort. Keep a diary. Put something in it everyday. Reflect. Even if it is only 20 minutes or half hour at a time but be honest.

5. Left-Hand Writing

This is a specialized technique of journaling. For people who are right-handed, using the left hand often allows them to come up with a whole bunch of memories that were previously undisclosed to them. It allows the vulnerable side of them, the beaten and bruised but courageous inner child, to speak. I have found this method of journaling extremely helpful for people to get in touch with previously undisclosed memories of trauma, especially physical abuse, incest, incestuous rape and ritualistic abuse.

6. Dream Work

Work through dreams, nightmares, fantasies, phobias and flashbacks. By this, I mean use dreams as a way of getting in touch with unconscious feelings and memories. What the mind cannot accept and deal with in reality and at a conscious level comes out in the form of dreams, nightmares, flashbacks, obsessive and phobic thoughts and uncontrollable daytime fantasies.

One patient, for example, when she made contact with her preacher about a particular problem that she was having in her marriage, made her sexually aroused. This then resulted in dreams of incest with her father. Dreams of sexual situations with parents or parent-like figures are important. Violent dreams—where you are hurting, killing or afraid of being hurt or killed—can be important and suggestive of a fearful childhood.

Lisa was a manager for a major department store chain. She did not complain of any depression or anxiety problems. She was a college graduate and had worked consistently after graduation. The only problems that she had were those related to anorexia nervosa—gastrointestinal problems. She also had a history of chronic pelvic cysts. At times she would feel extremely weak. She had a history of hypotension (low blood pressure) and fainting spells.

By the time she came into the hospital, in addition to anorexia, she became extremely depressed. She said being in the hospital was depressing. For four months, I would see her every day. She would sit in the chair and say nothing. She would be almost catatonic at times. I did all the talking.

Four months into therapy she started remembering a dream in which she was in a bus with another little girl and a boy who were her classmates at the time she was in the sixth or seventh grade. I then started doing hypnosis, and that allowed her to recall an incident when she was in the sixth or seventh grade, when she and two of her friends would take off with this guy who befriended them outside the school yard and who would buy them a number of presents like sweets, roller skates and toys. He would take them into his van. He would watch them in sexual acts he instructed them to do while he would masturbate. She then started remembering incidents that had to do with her brother's physically and sexually abusing her. He would also call his friends while he was supposed to be babysitting her and then join them in abusing her sexually. They would treat her like a slave after tying her up.

All this happened before she was eight years old. It continued until she was in her early teens. All of these memories came up during the last two months of her hospitalization. Up to that time, she had been completely blocked. Almost six months after she left the hospital, she began to have flashbacks and recall of things that happened between her and her father. She began to remember how her father had raped her repeatedly as well as having a circle of his friends rape her when she was 12 years old. One might think that this was the end of her history of abuse and that there could be nothing more to be asked. But one never knows; as therapists we keep on thinking and asking about further possibilities and, even then, sometimes we just have to "wait it out."

I found this out at a time while she was still in therapy with me. She came to me with a letter that her father had sent her, giving her some money and asking her to book a motel room for them. Through this, I found that even up to six months before she actually came to the hospital, he had still been having sex with her.

It is hard to say what may have been remembered and what may have been forgotten, especially for people who suffer from dissociative disorders. You have to keep in mind the possibility that you never know all the things that have happened to you. You need to continuously take inventory and do memory work so that what you feel, think and act in your day-to-day life is always connected to things in the past and, thus, makes sense.

Jean, a 34-year-old married co-dependent, had a history of depression and sexual dysfunction. "Whey my husband has sex without foreplay, I have fantasies of sex with my father, and this will freeze up my body. I'll be like sort of paralyzed. I'll just wait until he is done." She recalled incest memories by hypnosis. Her father would come up to her when she was sleeping and urge her to be quiet. He would remind her of this by putting his palm over her mouth to prevent her from making noises while he had sex with her forcibly.

Certain situations in people cause intense fear and physical symptoms, physical pain and discomfort. This means something subconscious is being triggered—a sign that you need to think more about it instead of pushing it out of your mind or going out and having a drink.

Lillian hated to go into the gym. (I had told her to work out as a way to fight depression.) "I don't know why I feel this way. My legs shake and get wobbly in the dressing room. I get sweaty. My heart pounds like it is going to come out of my chest. I feel like I want to go the bathroom. I get lightheaded. I feel scared and ashamed."

Under hypnosis, Lillian recalled a molestation that occurred when she was in elementary school during which time a female physical education teacher molested her for an entire year in the locker room, a memory that she had completely blocked.

7. Flashbacks

While flashbacks are uncomfortable, distracting, confusing and often frightening, my advice to people all the time is that you should feel blessed if you have flashbacks. You must, like other signals from your repressed and forgotten memories of the past, think about them as a scream for help—a reaching out of the child within.

Instead of running away or blocking the flashbacks, look at them, feel them, "tease" them out. If they are single-frame pictures, try to identify what is in the picture—like a scene frozen on the screen of your video player; scary or disgusting as it may be, you want it played forward and backward, in slow motion, while you remember, think and feel. Get in touch with it.

Karen, a 39-year-old interior decorator, a cocaine and "speed" addict, had her nine-year-old son under my care for depression, suicidal feelings and behavior problems at school. She called me after a meeting earlier in the evening. She was sobbing and hyperventilating on the phone. It was easy to recognize that she was very distraught.

Earlier in the evening I had informed her that her son told me his biologic father, separated from his mother, had sexually abused him—committed fellatio and sodomized him between the ages of four and six when his father moved out of the home.

The patient was rightfully angry, concerned, feeling sad for her son and guilty that maybe she should have somehow prevented it.

On her way home, still thinking about what we had discussed, a single visual frame "exploded in my mind," she said. "I felt my heart skip a beat—I felt like I was punched in the stomach, like the air went out of my lungs. I gripped the steering wheel like I was going to pass out. I knew I was going to crash. At the same instant, I felt like I was going to throw up. I felt I could not control my bladder and rectum. I wet myself in the same instant. I regained control, feeling the seat to be wet.

"I felt humiliated and confused. I rolled down the window because I felt sick and weak. What had flashed through my mind was a picture of my father—not as he is now but as he was when I was a child, in his boxer shorts, looking down at me. I tried to distract myself, turned up the volume of the music in my car, looked at passing cars, opened and closed the window but in spite of all this, the picture would push itself into my head momentarily, then disappear. This happened continuously.

"I prayed. Nothing would make it go away. I somehow got home and went into the shower to clean up. As I turned on the shower, I started shaking as though I was having a convulsion. I started retching violently. I could no longer stand up. I dropped to the floor of the shower, threw my arms around my knees, my head between my knees and started sobbing violently like a child. The water was burning my skin, I could see it grow red but I felt no pain."

Over the phone I asked Karen what she was thinking, what kind of mental pictures she was having. She described having flashbacks of her father in the shower.

Dr. Nair: *Close your eyes and tell me where he is standing.*
Karen: *He is standing with his back to the shower door.*
    N: *How about you?*
    K: *I'm under the shower.*
    N: *How old do you think you are? How tall do you think you are at this time?*
    K: *I'm about at his belly button, maybe four or five.* (She is sobbing, her voice is very shaky.)

N: *What happens next? What is he doing? Does he leave?*
     Does he come towards you? What does he do?

K: (Sobbing) *No, no, this cannot be true. Oh my God. This*
     can't be true.

N: *Tell me what you think is happening. Tell me just like you*
     are watching it on TV. Just keep on letting it play. Don't
     struggle with trying to ask yourself whether this is real or
     not real. Don't struggle in trying to think whether this a
     bad dream or a fantasy. Keep your eyes closed if it helps.
     Just tell me what you see.

K: *He is taking his thing out of his boxer shorts.*

N: *Which hand is he using?*

K: *His left hand.*

N: *What is he doing next?*

K: *He is rubbing it. He is making it big.*

N: *What are feeling? What are you thinking?*

K: *I'm scared. It doesn't feel right . . . I'm shaking. It doesn't*
     feel right . . . I'm scared.

N: *What does he do next?*

K: *He grabs my head and pulls me towards his belly. He is*
     trying to push his thing into my mouth. He is grabbing
     me by the hair. I feel like my neck is breaking. Oh, my
     God (tremendous sobbing)! He is forcing his penis inside
     my mouth. He is pressing my head against his belly with
     both his hands. He is moving his hips. I feel like I'm
     choking. I can't breathe. His whole body is shaking. I feel
     numb. Then he is done: "You made your Daddy very
     happy. Don't tell Mommy. It's our secret." He left the
     shower. I sat on the floor of the shower with my arms
     around my knees, my head down. I was sobbing.

     I felt dirty. I felt sick. I could still feel him holding my
     head against his belly, hearing the noises that he made. I
     felt dirty. I'm dirty. I washed and washed until my skin
     was red and raw.

The patient recalls crying into her pillow that night. "I felt terribly lonely." She knew she had done something wrong. She couldn't go to her mother.

"He had bathed me, touched me between my legs before. I didn't think that there was anything wrong but this was different. I wanted to die. I felt ashamed. I felt angry. I kept thinking of him doing it to me. I couldn't get it out of my mind.

"I felt nervous at breakfast. My father did not say anything. He acted like he usually did at breakfast, like nothing had happened."

Over a six-month period, through hypnosis and journaling, she recovered more memories, memories of him molesting her over and over again, having her stay away from school, raping her many times when her mother was away at work.

"This stopped when I started having menses at the age of 12."

At the age of 15 Karen got into drugs. Her father beat her up when she started dating a same-age peer. He called her a slut. She overdosed at the age of 15 and was hospitalized in a psychiatric hospital for three weeks. She said nothing about the abuse.

"The doctor was a friend of the family." Her father was a dentist in a small town.

A life of drugs, running away and a marriage at the age of 17 followed. She had three marriages, all to physically and sexually abusive alcoholic men—sexual addicts.

Her father sent her money when she occasionally asked for help.

She was 39 years old when she started in therapy with me. She had an I.Q. of 126 and three and a half years of college; she just could not get herself to complete it. She was good at her job but held back her successes. She had abused cocaine, alcohol and amphetamines in the past.

Through therapy, 12-Step work and body work, she is finally seeing a light at the end of the tunnel. She reported her son's father to the Child Protective Services.

At my advice, we met with her brother and sent the letter with the facts, confronting her father. She is suing him for damages.

8. Exploring Body Memories

The body carries the wounds of childhood long after the mind has blocked it out.

Jane remembers: "My first recollection of abuse came when I visited a gynecologist because I had pelvic inflammatory disease and pelvic cysts which caused me pain. I was 29 and had never been sexually active, never masturbated. I remembered nothing of my childhood and little of my teenage years. My life began as I recalled it when I moved out of the home of my parents after I completed school. I didn't like my parents and when I visited them—rarely—I felt extremely uncomfortable in their presence. I hated him [her father] touching me and I thought I would explode when he did that. I would get sick. I would think I was a bad person

because I couldn't love them. I would become suicidal after these
visits home. I would feel like hurting myself, like cutting on myself.
  The gynecologist told me that I had lots of scars in my vagina. He
was puzzled because I told him I was a virgin and that I did not
masturbate, an explanation that he suggested for causing these scars.
From that point the patient began to have intense memories and
flashbacks—memories of incest and ritual abuse, gang rape by father, uncles and friends of the father.
  Body work, massage and hypnosis brought out more and more
memories of being tied down and gang raped ceremonially, being
involved in infant sacrifices, of blood smeared all over her body, of
men in dark robes around her, and of being drugged.
  When touched during body work around her ankles and her
wrists, she would start screaming. Her back would become stiff like
a board that was about to crack.
  She had fought 12 years of feeling suicidal, endured self-mutilation, anorexia and bulimia, severe abdominal and pelvic pain and
migraine headaches.
  She is bright and strong, well dressed and seemingly confident
looking, not at all like someone you would expect with such a
horrendous past. She is a survivor.
  "I'd go to bed feeling fine; I'd wake up in the morning in a dark
cloud, wanting to die and I wouldn't know why. It is slowly beginning to come together."
  Ken, a 35-year-old alcoholic, never had been married and had
never been sexually active. He came to me because of severe depression and because he was not able to control his diabetes. He
was also impotent. He had been sober three years and attended AA
regularly. He was very religious. He could not understand why he
was so unhappy.
  A detailed history revealed a background of alcoholic parents—
a father who abandoned him at the age of three and a stepfather
who physically abused him and his mother and his two sisters. Both
his sisters have depression and eating disorders. He did not know if
his sisters were sexually abused (when I questioned him about
this) but his stepfather was suddenly put out of the house when he
was 12 years old. This happened after his stepfather violently beat
up one of his sisters after she had dated a boy.
  His stepfather regularly referred to his sisters as "slut" and
"whore." He referred to all the females in the household as "cunts"
when he talked to Ken about them.

During body work therapy, pressure on his calves brought up for the first time intense picture memories: "I'm about six or seven. A man in cowboy boots and jeans and a checked shirt carries me from the living room to the bedroom.

"I think he's a neighbor, maybe a friend of my father's. My mother is at work. He is taking care of me. He flopped me on my belly and pulled my pants down. I hear him unbuckle his belt. I brace myself, clutching the sheets with my hands, waiting to feel the strap on my buttocks as my stepfather did when he was mad. Mostly, I didn't know why I would get beaten." The patient felt he was going to be whipped, although he did not know why.

"I felt the pressure—pain on my calves. His legs were on my calves, pinning me down. I felt something between my buttocks. I felt his body on me, his chest on my back, pressing me down. I could feel the heat and the sound of his breathing on my head and my neck. I don't remember what happened but I was squirming and he put a pillow over my head and held it down . . . it gets blurry."

"I remember being alone after he got off, with an incredible feeling of shame. I don't know if he sodomized me. I knew I had been bad. I knew I was dirty. I knew I could not tell anyone."

9. Talking To Relatives, Siblings, Parents, Grandparents, Uncles And Family Friends

I will warn you ahead of time that it may be extremely traumatic to do this. On the other hand it might trigger off thoughts and feelings that you need to deal with. For many, it is an absolute step toward self-empowerment to make this contact and to be able to live through it and to go beyond it.

Going through the photo albums of childhood, visiting your old school, driving around in your old neighborhood, talking to classmates—all of this can help.

10. Psychotherapy

Working in therapy gives you a chance towards increased self-observation. A good therapist can often help you get in touch with memories but it is important that both you and the therapist focus towards doing this. It is very common for many therapists to tell their patients that they mustn't think about their past. This is dangerous advice.

11. Hypnosis

Hypnosis can be of tremendous help, cutting down the time of traditional psychotherapy by months and years. It is important to choose a hypnotherapist that you can trust. It is good to get second and third opinions. "Shop around" before you choose one. If there is no movement in therapy after months, it is wise to consider making a change. It may be helpful to tape the hypnotherapy sessions and listen to them several times during the week in a "safe" place while massaging yourself and feeling soothed or while exercising to help you get in touch and to hold onto the feelings and memories brought up during the hypnosis sessions. These then need to be worked through in the psychotherapy sessions and in groups and 12-Step meetings.

Many therapists and psychiatrists have often told patients that regressive therapies such as hypnosis and body work should not be done because they may remember "too much" and that they are "not prepared for it." My question is, when is a person finally going to deal with traumatic memories that hold them back and cause them pain everyday in their life and in their relationships? When are they supposed to begin to leave the nightmare behind? When can they be free? When can they start living their own lives and dreaming their own dreams?

I have seen people who have been in conventional therapy for two years and I have seen people who have been in therapy for 20 years without making any movement, continuing to be tormented by chronic depression, lack of self-esteem, self-hate, self-mutilation and multiple suicide attempts, living on in co-dependent relationships, relapsing into drugs, alcohol and other chemical addictions.

I feel glad for the motivated patient who is doing honest 12-Step work, who has attempted psychotherapy, who exercises, does other self-soothing methods such as biofeedback, and when these things have been tried, goes on to more intense methods to increase self-awareness and memory recall such as by hypnosis and body work.

A significant and often dramatic resolution of their symptoms comes about by these methods.

I feel sad for people who have lived to be 50 and 60 years old, carried the sickness of co-dependency, addictions and abuse into the second and third generation who still cannot remember where their anguish and their shame came from.

I feel that for such people it is absolutely essential that every effort to recall their childhood should be attempted.

Desiree came to me because of cocaine addiction problems and depression. The staff saw her as being a "borderline personality disorder." During her first hospitalization and the outpatient treatment that followed, she got in touch with memories of having been sexually abused by her stepfather. Two years later, the patient, after having shown some recovery and continuing to work, once again became seriously suicidal in the context of a relationship in which she was the abusive person and had become violent towards her boyfriend, attempting to kill him by ramming his car with her car. She was once again back into alcohol and cocaine. She felt intensely suicidal.

During the second hospitalization which followed, effort was made through hypnosis and body work. Through the hypnosis the patient remembered much for the first time. She became aware that she had attempted suicide at the age of 18 while she was living on her own in Florida, when she was air-lifted to a medical surgical hospital after she overdosed on a potentially dangerous antidepressant, Parnate. She recalled a marriage that lasted approximately a year from which she had walked out. The marriage had been with a nonabusive male whom she had emotionally abused. When the patient suspected that he was having an affair, she walked out of his life and blotted the whole thing out of her mind.

She remembered incestuous sexual abuse by her mother's brother who raped her violently when was three or four years old. This appears to have been the major trauma which she had not been able to remember or work through. This had happened in her maternal grandmother's home and seemingly with the consent and knowledge of her grandmother. She remembered in a shocked-like state at the age of four reaching out to get to the tap in an attempt to wash the blood away from between her legs after her uncle had raped her and left her alone after he was done.

The patient continues to be very symptomatic. Although somewhat better, she refuses to attend 12-Step meetings and Incest Survivor meetings, to exercise or to obtain body work therapy. I believe this is the reason for her slow progress.

FOURTEEN

Healing The Mind
• Grief Work
• Rage Work
• Learning To Play

There is grief and rage in all adult children of dysfunctional families. They stuff it and hide it, often even from themselves. There is denial, repression and dissociation. All adult children who are not able to feel connected and healthy, who shortchange themselves, have grief and rage work that is unfinished. So, too, is the "work" of play unfinished in those who were denied the carefree dreaming and enjoyments of a healthy childhood.

Residual Grief From Infancy

Grief is the feeling that comes from losing love. The strongest and earliest sense of love comes from interactions between an infant and its mother. Therefore, maternal loss by death and abandonment are the most traumatic losses a child can undergo. However, absence, physical unavailability (as when a mother is sick and bedridden) and emotional unavailability all feel like losses to an infant whose sense of permanence, of *being* is not as strong as that of an adult.

Says one child specialist[1] of children from age 18 to 24 months: "If a child is taken from his mother's care at this age, when he is so possessively and passionately attached to her, it is indeed as if his world has been shattered. His intense need of her is unsatisfied, and the frustration and longing may send him frantic with grief. It takes an exercise of the imagination to sense the intensity of this distress. He is as overwhelmed as any adult who has lost a beloved person by death. To the child of two with his lack of understanding and complete inability to tolerate frustration, it is really as if his mother had died. He does not know death, but only absence; and if the only person who can satisfy this imperative need is absent, she might as well be dead, so overwhelming is his sense of loss."

Classic of a grief-filled infancy in childhood is one where the mother is always or often physically sick; always or often depressed, anxious, psychotic, or rageful and therefore, inconsistently or always unavailable. An alcoholic or a chemically-dependent mother or a mother who is often or always loaded up on prescription medications in essence abandons a child emotionally and physically. Such situations are chronic in the lives of adult children of alcoholics. An adult child of an alcoholic has many things to grieve about:

1. Loss of consistent maternal affection.
2. Loss of protection by mother/parents.
3. Loss of a protective and idealized mother when she is seen by the child to be abused and beaten in front of them by the male parent.
4. Loss of father because of drinking, absence and being emotionally unavailable or negative (anger/depression) even when the father is present.
5. Loss of the protective unit of mother/father when idealized parents separate or divorce. A child may act out or emotionally continue as if they are together instead of mourning such a loss.
6. Loss of idealized childhood that never was.
7. Loss of masculinity as when a child feels castrated when he is not able to save his beloved mother from the beatings of his father.
8. Loss of femininity when a female child watches her mother being abused and degraded for being a woman and being called names such as "bitch," "whore" and "cunt" or even "stupid."

The problem is that in alcoholic and other dysfunctional families a child is not allowed to mourn the losses. The adults are too busy, too crazy, too silly, too angry, too sad, too drunk, too sick, too stoned or simply not there to hear the sobbing. They have not been there to see your tears or simply sit down with you while you can allow yourself to be sad. No, you have to stuff it, forget it, deny it, let it become a stomach ache, an asthma attack, a headache; wet your bed with fear, bust someone else's window or someone else's nose. Then, you might be heard.

Repressed Grief Surfaces As Rage

Not being able to do appropriate mourning in childhood is the cause of both grief and rage.

A good rule of thumb is that usually- or always-depressed people need to get in touch with rage and work through it. People who are easily or always rageful need to get in touch with grief.

Most adult children of alcoholics need to do both grief and rage work.

Rage and grief work can be done by oneself, in groups, in trauma-specific 12-Step meetings and in individual therapy.

12-Step meetings that are specific to your hurt will help you to both remember and work through the pain and anger. Taking inventory, making a list of losses, a "hit list" of people and events that have hurt you, shamed you and put fear into you are both helpful and necessary.

Specialized techniques such as psychodrama and inner child work are helpful where traditional psychotherapy has failed. Find a resource for this. Using soft clubs (batakas), hitting a punching bag and screaming into a pillow, can all help you deal with some of the building anger that occurs when you start recognizing how it hurt you and how you were hurt.

Massage, being held, being heard as in a 12-Step meeting with people of a similar wounding or talking to sponsors can all help you to *grieve and mourn appropriately. Most of all you have to use your God-given mind and your imagination.*

In your imagination, you can fight back or confront those people who hurt or shamed you and were not there for you when you were a child.

You can kick them, hit them, scream at them, poke out their eyes, kick them in their testicles, cut off their penises, cut off their heads, strangle them as they strangled and suffocated you.

I often empower women who have been raped with a piece of information that I learned when I was training as a surgeon—a male with an erection can literally have his penis pulled off with a hard tug or "fractured" by forcible bending.

You can put before you a picture of yourself as a child and talk to him or her. Hold yourself, stroke yourself, allow the memories to come in, allow yourself to cry. You can visualize going to your hidden child and kneeling beside her—put an arm around her, hold her, put her head in your lap, stroke her, comfort her, close your eyes, let her cry, sob and scream. Compliment her on her courage, beauty, purity, goodness and her glory.

You can help as no one else can help. Search out the pain. Stay in touch. There is no other way. No short cuts.

Learning To Play

For those who have grown up in the warm and protective love of parents who loved and respected themselves and each other, childhood is full of wonder and magic. Truly, they will have seen "heaven in a blade of grass." Your back yard, trees, plants, flowers, birds, critters, bugs and butterflies, logs, pebbles and seashells, sunlight playing on water, the earth and the sky are your glorious playground. Crushing bugs, breaking things, building things, socializing—you learn about your power, your powerlessness, order and chaos, defeat and victory, about yourself and about others.

In play, the child learns to laugh, to deal with disappointments, to win, to fall, to be creative, to feel herself or himself the master or mistress of all they survey. In play, a child learns to dream and make his dreams real. A child that learns to play (and all children given the chance will learn to play) will become an adult who is able to relax, have fun and work creatively and to feel self-sufficient. In short, not to become co-dependent or addicted.

Adult children of dysfunctional families have been robbed of childhood and have not learned to play. They have not been allowed to dream. They have only been allowed to live someone else's nightmare. They have not had a chance to connect to the universe around them, big or small—to get pleasures from the simple things and simple events that childhood is so full of. Sometimes they have simply not been allowed the time. Between the loneliness, self-pity and the consuming rage and hopelessness of an abandoned child or having to worry about an incompetent, affectionless parent, there is not time to play; or play becomes something to please parents by being "perfect" at some activity or as a means to manipulate parents but simply not for oneself.

Adult children of dysfunctional families, co-dependents and addicts have a big part of themselves missing here in development and this makes them not be able to keep themselves excited, self-soothed or provide for themselves "safe spaces" among the day-to-day stressors of life. So they run towards addictions and co-dependency.

Steps In Learning To Play

1. Take the time for Number One. Set aside an hour a day, a couple of days a week, a few weeks a year for playing. This is one of the things that I absolutely insist on for people in recovery.
2. Establish hobbies and don't make your hobbies into work or something intensely competitive that is no longer fun.
3. It is more important to play yourself rather than watching others play.
4. For those who are used to ruminating, dissociating and living in their heads (intellectualization), play that incorporates their body is essential. Body surfing, swimming, walking vigorously, walking through the woods, camping, hiking, climbing, cycling, river rafting will all allow you to get in touch with your visceral self—your lungs, heart, muscles and skin. Such play puts you in touch with the joy and glory of nature that surrounds us—the wind, the waves, ocean and mountains, plants and other creatures in God's "glorious dream." It gives you the kind of comforting and excitement and connectedness that you may not have gotten from your family.

   Co-dependents and addicts are compulsive about recovery. They want to do it all in one day and all the time. They want to read every self-help book, lap up every seminar until they feel overwhelmed, numbed or simply relapse into chemicals, relationships, eating and work.

   Sometimes, many times, the most important part of recovery may be taking the time to play.

---

1. Robertson, J. "A Guide to the Film: A Two Year Old Goes to Hospital." London: Tavistock Child Development Research Unit, Third Edition, 1965.

FIFTEEN

Choosing
A Therapist

Let me start out by emphasizing that among co-dependents, abuse survivors, addicts and other people coming from dysfunctional family environments that are secretive, shaming, abandoning and discounting, psychotherapy *should not* be the primary approach to recovery.

Self-help through the self-healing methods described and discussed earlier and an honest working of trauma-specific 12-Step groups is the number one treatment. I don't believe that a person can really be in recovery if they only go and see a therapist but will not attend 12-Step meetings. That would be a caricature of therapy.

Adults from dysfunctional families often make bad choices of therapists; as in their other relationships, they may make a choice of a therapist for all the wrong reasons and without the capacity to examine why.

Anna provides an example. "I stayed for three years in therapy with Dr. X because he told me that I was one of his three best patients." At the end of that time she stopped abruptly because she saw her male therapist linger on at the door of the consulting room with another attractive female patient and this therapist did not acknowledge or make eye contact with her. She immediately flew into a terrible rage because she felt that she had been dropped from the favored position of being one of his three best patients.

Because patients who come from a background of abuse have a need to put someone above them to give them the answers, appropriate expressions of helplessness on the therapist's part may make such a patient, instead of looking into themselves, simply leave the therapist. Such a patient may not like a therapist because he or she does not have all the answers. A patient may shy away from the therapist who is honest and confrontive because he or she is beginning to weaken the armor of the patient's denial. They may be drawn to a therapist because he or she is a "friend" and one who does not confront acting out behaviors or "get on their case" about being apathetic or not attending 12-Step meetings. They may be drawn towards therapists who have endless time for them, without pausing to think that maybe the therapist is being enabling (promoting dysfunction).

Abuse survivors and co-dependents in therapy are more likely to get involved in sexual activity with the therapist than those who have not been abused. They may use sex as a way of proving to themselves that all men are like their fathers and other perpetrators. They may use sex as a way of reaffirming their false sense of self-esteem and their "sexual power." It may be a way for the patient to reach out because they know no other way.

Co-dependent patients have often been drawn into providing sex for older male therapists who let their patients know about their own loneliness and sadness.

One out of ten therapists rape their patients. Sometimes the patient may initiate it, just as a sexually abused, precocious six-year-old may start fondling an older male relative—but it is for the therapist (as it should have been for the older male) to set boundaries from the start.

The greatest danger for abuse survivors in therapy is the possibility of "endless therapy." Therapy that is enabling or abusive is done to make the therapist feel more important rather than help the patient.

A psychiatrist may abuse patients by giving them addictive or brain-damaging medications that cover up instead of help the patient get to the roots of problems and work through them.

Being Honest With Your Therapist

Craig was a 40-year-old male with a history of chronic depression. "My therapist slept through the entire session. He was actually snoring."

> *Dr. Nair: Why didn't you wake him up or leave?*
> *Craig: I didn't want to be rude.*

It is not a good start to be in therapy with a therapist who is bored, anxious or fearful for you. It is all right for you to have negative feelings towards the therapist. Sometimes it may be because he or she has done something truly upsetting, i.e., multiple cancellations or sleeping in sessions, that as an adult you need to confront them with. Often it may be because of unfinished business from your past, your hidden anger and your sense of betrayal by other parent-like figures in your life that you transfered onto your therapist. *Idealization and devaluation is the rule* in the lives of co-dependents. In fact, this is so predictable that I will tell patients all the time when they come into therapy that no matter how wonderful they may feel that I am at the onset of therapy, a time will come when they will spend much of their waking moments resenting me. In any case, it is important that you are totally honest about your feelings towards your therapist. It is the therapist's role to take care of himself or herself.

Male Therapist Or Female Therapist?

A *good* therapist is the answer. A lot of men who come from abusive, alcoholic homes may hesitate to go into therapy. Some will hesitate strongly to go to men because they remind them of their abusive male parent. They may go to women for the wrong reasons. If you have a problem with men, you need to talk about it in therapy, whether your therapist is a male or a female. It may sometimes be more helpful for starters for an incest survivor to go to a female therapist only because sitting in a closed room with a male therapist may be too threatening or distracting.

Donna was an incest survivor who came to me in a rage about the therapist I had assigned to her. "All I could see was the shape of his genitals through his pants. I felt that he was pushing it in my face in the way that he sat."

Good therapists are able to recognize safe distances, positioning their bodies relative to the patient's state of mind. A patient may hear from a good therapist such questions as what distance from the therapist does the patient feel safe. "Am I too close? Am I too far? Am I talking too loudly? Can you hear me well? Am I talking too fast? Am I talking too much?"

Such a therapist is caring without being enabling. This therapist is appropriately but not endlessly available, confrontive but not sadistic, loving but not seductive. Above all, challenging instead of saying, "uh, uh" or just nodding so as not to upset you. The goal of all individual therapists should be to help the person find their own inner strengths.

No therapist that is unwilling to encourage their patients towards self-help techniques and 12-Step attendance can truly be working for the patient's recovery.

My experience is that people even with very severe problems such as major depression, suicidal tendencies, self-mutilation, sexually deviant behavior, borderline personality disorder or eating disorder, should not be in therapy beyond a period of one year. That is, if they are doing the work of recovery in all areas that I have described. Questions must be asked about the therapy and the therapist if recovery is not happening in six months to a year.

This does not mean that a patient may not seek therapy after that time but if the person is not able to get beyond the sense that they cannot *survive* without the therapist, then therapy can be something that is destructive rather than constructive, and taking the person further and further away from recovery.

SIXTEEN

12 Steps
To Freedom

The journey of a thousand miles into recovery starts with the 12 Steps. *The 12 Steps are the "sword and the shield" of recovery.* Let me say it again as I have said it before many times in this book and elsewhere: as long as people live in shame, abuse themselves, abuse others, do not feel proud as we as children of God ought to feel, it needs to be said and repeated until it is heard by everyone. *There is no recovery without the 12-Step program.* It is an unending process that takes a person from enslavement to empowerment, wisdom and joy.

I have told many a patient and friend that it is better to teeter into a meeting, holding onto the walls if you have to, carrying a vomit bag, than to stay at home stone sober. Because if you don't attend meetings, the day will come when you will relapse. On the other hand, as long as you attend meetings, sooner or later your feet will carry you towards the path of recovery.

The 12 Steps

1. *We admitted we are powerless over our addictions, that our lives are unmanageable.* This is an admission that we have a problem. The problem may be alcohol, food, drugs, sex, gambling, work or addictive relationships. It means that before we try to untangle why this problem exists, we have to admit to its existence and the fact that it is causing us to become emotionally and physically unhappy, affecting our growth and possibly hurting others. *Co-dependents,* too, need to repeat this themselves to keep in touch with reality—to recognize that no amount of talking over the phone, staying up at night or screaming is going to change the other person's addiction.

An addict must admit to powerlessness over an addiction and that no amount of wishing, wanting and hoping is going to make alcohol and drugs less dangerous.

Look at the ocean and the waves, feel the wind. You have no more control over addictions than you do over earthquakes and tidal waves. Therapists need to confront themselves and their patients on this powerlessness. To recognize truly powerless conditions is the first step towards recognizing your real power. Not to do this is to continue to live in a delusion. You will be spending all your energy fighting it or giving in to it but never going anywhere, spinning your wheels in place or going backwards.

2. *Came to believe that a power greater than ourselves will restore us to sanity.* Atheist or believer, all of us at some level recognize a power in our lives that is greater than ourselves. Some of us will see it outside, some inside, some will see it in all things. It represents the strongest, bravest, kindest, most loving and glorious part of ourselves and others that nothing can destroy. I personally like to think about the higher power as God or Love because love is indestructible and everything happens in love. Without having received or given love, we will not have existed. Even the cruelest of us wish to be loved. Even the cruelest of us wish that their children will love them—*especially* the cruelest.

For all of us, there is a journey into the desert. There, beyond the abuse, the hate, the rage and the shaming of people is a YOU that no one can destroy and no one can shame and no one can abandon. Sometimes, the journey into the desert means having to hit the rock bottom of despair and hopelessness. When you are in despair, you will, when you take the time and stay focused, hear the voice of the little child inside you. Your inner child who withstood the pain, the humiliation, the neglect, the betrayal but stayed alive. Get in touch and stay in touch with that inner child because it carries the seed of your indestructible, spiritual self.

3. *Made a decision to turn our will and our lives over to the care of God as we understood Him or Her.* We make a decision to give the control of our will and our lives to be guided by our spiritual self—that part of us that is undefiled and undefilable, courageous, honest and loving.

4. *Made a searching and fearless moral inventory of ourselves.* St. Augustine said, "If thou shouldst say, 'It is enough, I have reached perfection,' all is lost. For it is the function of perfection to make one know one's imperfections."

This means assuming accountability for your feelings and actions now and in the past. I cannot emphasize taking inventory enough. Taking inventory means *knowing or working towards knowing* at any time why you feel the way you feel.

What does "fearless moral inventory" mean? For people *who are coming out from under the toxic cloud of a dysfunctional family, who may feel good for the wrong reasons and feel bad for the wrong reasons, every feeling, every action, every thought and every physical symptom, every sleepless night must be examined and connected. Not to do so is to not be in recovery.*

Taking inventory is part and parcel of being able to differentiate your feelings from the feelings of others, your boundaries from others' boundaries, your self from your family's toxic baggage.

When you are carrying a lot of feelings and memories of a painful kind, inventory-taking may be seemingly overwhelming, confusing and impossible. It will be easier to run towards well-oiled or destructive ways of dealing with it—denial, dissociation, acting out or going back into addictive substances, lifestyles and relationships. Therefore, inventory-taking has to be a continuous process, both in 12-Step meetings and outside. Go through your pain list, your shame list, your "hit list," your guilt list. Work on it every day in *bite-sized pieces.* Ask yourself why you didn't sleep well last night. Ask yourself why your head or your back hurts.

A word of caution. You need to take breaks to self-soothe, to play, to give yourself joy. *Only you can take care of that child within you.* If you don't take the time to massage yourself and play alongside inventory-taking (as many addicts and co-dependents looking for quick fixes in a compulsive, perfectionistic manner will tend not to do early in recovery), you will, without realizing, become overwhelmed and go back to destructive ways of dealing with life.

As you begin to work your way out of the bad dreams and the bad tapes that have stuck with you from having survived a dysfunctional family environment, you will find that inventory-taking *and* your life will become easier and more meaningful and you will feel less and less out of control.

Inventory taking is a lifelong process that takes a person from addictions to growth, wisdom and joy in a spiritual sense. Loving oneself, others and God leads to, in time, being able to feel glorious and loved.

5. *Admitted to God, to ourselves and to another human being the exact nature of our wrongs.* Shame and guilt and other feelings that lower ourselves in our own eyes cannot truly be resolved without disclosure to others who can understand and hopefully empathize. We cannot reclaim our innate sense of pride if we have to walk around knowing that if the other person *really knew* they would shun us like lepers. You've got to know that in your gut, in your heart, they will still embrace you. Only honest disclosures in a 12-Step meeting with people of a common wounding will get you there.

An alcoholic teacher, *Allan* spent a month in a hospital program after he became suicidal. The onset of his depression and self-hate came after he sexually abused his stepson. His stepson went on to disclose the abuse while he himself was admitted to a drug abuse program. Allan was admitted into an inpatient treatment program where he was told that he should not make disclosures about having molested his son because the others would not understand him and would shun him.

I told him that he had not even begun the task of recovery and that his entire hospitalization could only have made him sicker and more dishonest.

6. *We're entirely ready to have God remove all these defects of character.* Why do we push people away when we really want them to come close? Why do people, tense after a difficult day at work, initiate or work themselves into a quarrel with someone they love and end it by saying, "I don't care, I don't need you," when in fact at that moment what they really want to say is, "I have had a difficult day at work. I need some support. I need to be held. I need you."

This, like other false and confused behaviors, comes from the *false self,* created as an armor for having grown up in a dysfunctional, noncommunicative, secretive, cultlike family environment where the truth is not allowed to be spoken. This step is another reminder to recognize the false self from the true self, and to allow one's actions to be directed by the true self without fear of rejection and with the honesty to acknowledge one's vulnerability.

7. *Humbly asked Him/Her to remove our shortcomings.* This is at once an admission of shortcomings of character which is important to break down denial, as well as an acknowledgment that the false self cannot set them right. Only God, our Higher Power, our True Self, can set us in the right direction.

8. *Made a list of all people we have harmed and become willing to make amends to all of them.* List all the people in your life who have been hurt by your addictions—hurt by your inattention, self-ishness, maladaptive behavior, disrespect or actual physical and sexual abuse. Feel the hurt that you have caused them. Let them know that you have wronged them. Now. Not tomorrow. Begin to work on getting rid of the guilt that your false sense has accumulated. Begin to start at once in a relationship that is honest, caring and based on mutual respect.

Here is one way this can be expressed: "I realize that my (work-aholism/alcoholism/sexual addiction) caused me to hurt you, stifle your creativity. I will undertake as of this moment to be respectful, caring and honest. As of today, as of this moment."

9. *Made direct amends to such people whenever possible except when to do so would injure them or others.* Sometimes the actions of an honest, caring and respecting relationship and the process of making amends may be needed to precede mere admissions of wrongdoing. An admission of wrongdoing may only serve to get rid of some of the wrongdoer's guilt in a hypocritical manner.

For example, a person may decide to go and tell his wife, "I realize I have been abusive and disrespectful to you. I let you put me through (law school/medical school) even though I knew I really didn't care for you. Now I want to get honest. I would like for us to separate"—versus an acknowledgment to oneself such as, "I realize as of this day I have been manipulative, selfish and abusive towards my partner. I will as of this day treat him or her as another child of God with love and respect."

10. *Continued to take personal inventory and when we are wrong, promptly admit to it.* This step emphasizes the continuous, consistent and increasing role of inventory taking. The wrongdoing which may have been unrecognized at an earlier time in recovery may be admitted to and amended as soon as we recognize this. This step emphasizes the need for setting aside time on a daily basis or even on an hourly basis when mood swings, irritability, physical

symptoms and pain call for a need to self-examine, no matter how long you have been sober.

11. *Sought through prayer and meditation to improve our conscious contact with God as we understood Him/Her, praying only for the knowledge of His/Her will for us and the power to carry this out.* This step acknowledges and reaffirms on a weekly, daily and hourly basis our commitment to *continuously* enlarge the role of our spiritual self in our lives by prayer, meditation, inventory taking and the acknowledgment of powerlessness.

This is an endless step that takes you from recovery to growth to having an increasing sense of meaning, joy and connectedness in your life.

12. *Having had a spiritual awakening as a result of these steps, we try to carry this message to others and to practice these principles in all our affairs.* Glorious and growing with an increasing sense of balance, meaningfulness and joy by way of our spiritual recovery, we carry this message to others in a non-co-dependent, non-abusive, non-guilt-producing manner by our participation in 12-Step meetings and by living the 12 Steps.

SEVENTEEN

Family Business: Confrontation, Forgiveness And Letting Go

It is important to confront parents and relatives with your feelings as a part of your recovery, as a part of putting your toxic baggage where it belongs. When parents and step-parents are deceased or have moved away, it is still important to list the reasons why you feel the hurt and betrayal and talk about such feelings with great honesty in therapy to your sponsors and to people who are close to you in your life and in your 12-Step meetings, as well as with all your other healthy supports.

Don't forgive prematurely. Only through the process of honest self-searching, hearing the anguished cries and the screams of your hidden child and being in touch can you come to the next step of accepting what you cannot change. Again, accepting does not mean forgiving. Some of us have parents and step-parents who have played with us, respected us, taken us when we were children on their shoulders and showed us what a wonderful place the world is. Some of us have drunks, workaholics and sex addicts for parents and maybe in our own growth we may come to a point of forgiving them.

On the other hand, there are some of us who have been raped and seen our brothers and sisters raped, beaten and even killed at the hands of parents and it is not appropriate to expect that an individual will ever be able to forgive such a parent.

The important thing is to be able to forgive yourself for the negative feelings that you have harbored towards them, including hateful and murderous feelings, and to acknowledge that they gave you enough reason to have these feelings when you were a child. It is important that you do not intellectualize and explain away the harmful actions, the discounting, the betrayal and the abandonment of your childhood. Because what this means more than anything else is that you are abandoning the thoughts, feelings and experiences and the reality of your inner child.

Thinking, writing down and talking about the details of how you were abused, how you were wounded is important. Confronting your perpetrators is important as a step towards a more healthy relationship, if that can come about. *Otherwise, you will be living a lie.* If you find it difficult, picture your own child or a friend's child in your place. Ask yourself what kind of feeling you would have if you knew your father or mother treated them as they treated you. Visualize your father, now fat and benign-looking, in a drunken rage, lifting two-year-old "Erin" off the ground by her neck. Imagine him pushing his body against her. Then ask yourself if in fact you have forgiven.

The bottom line on how you deal with the family in recovery is as follows:

1. Be honest with your feelings towards them, past and present. Write down things that you want to confront them with if you choke up when you meet them and find it hard to talk. Your therapist should help bring about these meetings.
2. Let them *know* about your feelings. More often than not, breaking your denial will give them the opportunity to accept, feel and take responsibility and begin the process of making amends that will be an important step towards a more meaningful relationship and a truer sense of recovery in themselves.
3. If they continue to remain in denial, you need to move on while coming to terms with your feelings of anger, abandonment and sadness. Acknowledge your powerlessness in not being able to change them.
4. You cannot work on your own recovery if you continue to remain enmeshed with family members who are not in recovery.

Elaine is a woman I came to know when she was hospitalized under my care for manic-depressive illness about eight years ago. She made me aware that her mother also suffered from manic-depressive illness and that her father had been an alcoholic who was periodically sober but continued to drink for the most part. She felt that they controlled her life and her solution was to move from California to Colorado. However, her mood swings and depression were only temporarily resolved. She was rehospitalized in a crisis situation three years later. I insisted on having a family meeting. By this time, the patient had become increasingly in touch with painful memories of living with an alcoholic sexual addict father and a co-dependent mother. She was fully able to confront them.

Moving away from parents with whom you have an enmeshed, abusive relationship is not the answer. It is confronting and dealing with the feelings within yourself that is most important.

EIGHTEEN

Psychiatric Illness: Myth And Reality

Freedom is about having choices. This chapter is meant to empower you with the knowledge that will help you to look at choices. It is not meant to put down one discipline or another.

I suggest that people who have been diagnosed as having major depression, manic-depressive illness, schizophrenia and anxiety-panic-phobic disorders read this section carefully. These people have often been assured by their doctors and therapists that they may have a genetic or a medical illness for which medications are the only way to recovery.

Forty-five million Americans are diagnosed at some time as being mentally ill. Let us take a look at mental illness.

Psychiatric illness or "medical psychiatric illness" or "biologic mental disorders" are terms still somewhat inaccurate since there is no *inherited mental illness* as one can describe Huntington's Chorea or hemophilia where a person has a 50/50 or a one-in-four chance towards having the illness if one of the parents has it.

A person can be at greater risk because of genetic factors. Depression, mood swings, alcoholism and suicide run high in families of co-dependents and addicts. It is true that in some instances a genetic proneness ("loading") towards depression can co-exist and make the person even more vulnerable in recovery and that in some instances medications may indeed be helpful.

Does this mean, however, that these people are carrying "bad genes?" Does this mean that they should never get married, never have children? Does it mean that people should not have a relationship with them? Does it mean that they must stay medicated for the rest of their lives because they're stricken with an "illness" and they have a "defect" (like webbed toes and fingers or cystic fibrosis)? The answer, clearly, is no. There is no mental disorder that karyotyping (identifying chromosomes) will help identify and label as one can identify and label a disorder like Down's syndrome (mongolism). There is no chemical test that will identify a "mental illness" as one can identify clearcut genetic disorders such as phenylketonuria (PKU) or Huntington's disease. Even a PET scan that will show the workings of the living brain will not "diagnose" depression or other mental illness.

It is important to have knowledge about these psychiatric labels so you are empowered to make your own decisions, read and get second opinions rather than simply take medications or accept a diagnosis because your doctor tells you so.

"Out of Sync"

An increasing awareness of Western medicine, long accepted in Eastern medicine, is that disease comes when man is "out of sync." Out of synchronization with himself, his family, his society and nature. The rhythms within the body of cells, hormones, digestive, cardiac and other functions go "out of whack" and produce disease. The person needs to be in sync with the outside. The mind needs to be in sync with the body. Failure of any of these leads to diseased states of body and mind.

For some people, being out of sync, being out of touch with themselves, causes addictions and co-dependency; for others, it causes gastric ulcers, mood swings, psoriasis and nightmares. It is getting to understand why you are out of synch that may be the most important part of getting better from emotional and physical problems.

Our increasing understanding of the connections between the mind and the brain, the endocrine, the immune and the nervous system, clearly lead us in this direction.

It is a common and dangerous pitfall that everyone, especially people from a dysfunctional family background, who is easily indoctrinated and already in a mode of thinking about "outside fixes" think there is only one way and that one way may be medications. That somehow, somewhere, there is a pill or a shot that will make everything better.

Following is a review of the three major groups of psychiatric illnesses.

Psychiatric Illnesses And Their Symptoms

Depression

Major depressive disorder, dysthymic disorder and unipolar depression are the most common of "mental disorders." They are diagnosed in one-fourth of all females and one-tenth of all men in this country. The symptoms are intense and prolonged—weeks, months and years. These include feeling sad, hopeless, helpless, guilt-ridden, irritable with disturbed sleep (too much or too little sleep), disturbed appetite (too much or too little), disturbance of attention and concentration and loss of interest or pleasure in activities that are normally enjoyed. Recurrent thoughts of death or suicide, wishing to die or making suicide attempts may be present. Distracted and disturbed thinking includes paranoia, hearing voices that say bad and angry things or tell persons to do harmful things to themselves (command hallucinations). Preoccupation with bodily sickness may also be present as a part of major depression.

While genes can carry an illness through generations, so can learned behaviors. We know that depression and suicide run in families but to what degree it is, nature (genetic) or nurture (learned within the family system) is not at all clear.

Antidepressants used for treating major depression can be uncomfortable, unsafe and often don't work. For details, see the section on medications.

Electro-Convulsive Therapy (ECT) is another oversold "quick fix" that is increasingly making a comeback for treating depression in this country. It has a long history of being abused. ECT has a history just like tranquilizers, like Thorazine, to be used more for people whose behavior causes a problem for the people around them than for the person themselves. However, its current use in depression can only be done with the patient's full willingness and the agreement of several doctors who feel it is appropriate.

The common factor to both antidepressants and electro-convulsive therapy (ECT) is that they don't cure and can often be a crutch that leads abuse survivors away from true recovery and, like all other crutches, can be dangerous.

Abuse survivors, addicts and co-dependents have plenty of reason to feel depressed, both in their present life and from things in their past. Getting to the roots of the depression, shame, self-disgust, self-hate and guilt through a 12-Step recovery program, and working through the feelings and memories is the only way towards long-term recovery and growth.

Depression weakens you and makes it difficult to think and act and be motivated. Sometimes a walking stick or a crutch can help you go uphill or on difficult terrain. However, if you are balancing a load of toxic baggage, you need to get rid of that first before you reach out for the crutches. You will find almost always that you really don't need the crutches. If you do decide to take medications and other approaches are being tried simultaneously, it is important to get off as soon as possible, as you become stronger through the honest working of the 12 Steps.

Manic-Depressive Illness/Bipolar Disorder

According to the American Psychiatric Association, *manic-depressive illness* or *bipolar disorder,* as it is currently called, affects one in every one hundred people and is manifested by sharp mood swings with periods of normal moods in between. The symptoms of mania (the "up" phase) include feeling unrealistically and excessively "good" (euphoria), grandiose feelings, hyperactivity with excessive plans of participating in numerous seemingly creative activities that have a good chance for painful results.[1]

Patients jump from one idea to another with loud rapid speech, sometimes to the point of becoming incoherent. They may feel no need for sleep for days at a time. When confronted, they may go from feeling grandiose, godlike and euphoric to becoming irritable, angry, rageful and overtly paranoid. Hypersexuality, excessive work and violent behavior may all be seen. This phase may last for days or weeks and then becomes normal in mood or depressed with helpless, hopeless and suicidal feelings and intense feelings of lethargy.

Manic-depressive illness is reported as being strongly genetically influenced. It is safe to assume that manic-depressive illness does exist. But what percentage of people who carry the "genes" of manic-depressive illness, no one really knows. On the other hand, psychiatrists and psychologists will treat any person who complains of mood swings as if they have manic-depressive illness.

In a study of "normal kids," i.e., adolescents randomly chosen as opposed to being referred for psychiatric or behavioral problems, psychologists identified symptoms of manic-depressive illness in one out of seven of these adolescents. This becomes the basis for looking into medication alternatives.

It is the tendency to over-identify, arbitrarily identify and medicate people rapidly for mood swings that clearly poses a danger. This is especially true for the recovering community of addicts and co-dependents because almost 100 percent of them will have mood swing problems. Most adults from dysfunctional families are holding onto a lot of anger and sadness from childhood and can alternate between periods of time when they push it deeper and convince themselves that everything is okay or even "fine." They may even party heavily and seem very excited, sometimes unbearably so, by others. They may be driven into hedonistic pursuits that often look like mania. They may sexually "act out" and be deemed as "hyper-sexual" when in fact the problem may be a premature and excessive investment in sexual feelings resulting from childhood sexual trauma. When denial, repression and dissociation fail, such people will go into a depressed state.

Manic-depressive illness is treated with Lithium and neuroleptic medication (Haldol, Thorazine, Mellaril, Stelazine, Moban, Prolixin and Loxitane, among others). More recently other medications such as Tegretol (an anticonvulsant) and Isoptin (a calcium channel blocker) have been used. These medications will be discussed more extensively later.

Anxiety Disorders

Panic disorders, phobias and obsessive-compulsive disorders are the signs of anxiety—the feelings of fear or worry along with the feeling that "something bad" will happen to you and your loved ones. Bodily sensations include feeling dizzy, shaky, sweaty, pounding and racing of the heart, feeling faint, dry mouth, numbness and tingling around the mouth, hands and feet. A person may feel like they are going to lose control of their bladder and bowel. Hyperventilation, shortness of breath, choking and gasping sensations may be present. An intense and unbearable sense of dread makes a person feel like they're losing control, like they're going crazy.

Anxiety disorders are suffered by between 5.1 to 12.5 percent of the population—by about 25 million people in America.

Phobias are one type of anxiety disorder where certain situations and activities, things or persons can cause intense fear and the symptoms described above to the point where the person will go out of their way to avoid such an activity or situation. It can cause sufferers to avoid people, to be confined to their homes, to stop driving and to stop working. Sometimes innocent situations like seeing a snake, being in public, being in the open, going up an escalator and driving, can cause deadly terror. The person is not able to talk themselves out of it. It can be a lifelong and worsening disorder.

Panic disorder affects 1.2 million people and differs from phobia in a sense that though the bodily symptoms—

Sweating
Heart pounding
Hot flashes
Trembling
Shortness of breath
Choking
Chest tightness
Faintness
Feelings of losing control
Feeling like you're going to explode
Feeling like you're going to die
Feeling that you are going crazy

—may be similar, the sufferer does not have a trigger as in a phobia.

Severe depression, suicide, alcohol abuse and the abuse of prescription medications are serious complications of people who suffer from anxiety, phobia and panic disorders.

Obsessive-compulsive disorder affects 2.4 million Americans. These individuals deal with anxiety by ritual behavior such as handwashing to the point that the hands are bleeding; housecleaning for hours or having to return 30 times back to the house before going on a trip to make sure that the door is locked or that the gas is turned off. An example is Howard Hughes and his obsessive preoccupation with germs.

Obsessive disorders are preoccupation with words and thoughts, mental pictures that continuously come into the mind and cannot be shaken off. They may be violent, sexual or distasteful because they're tabooed or shameful. Religious or anti-religious thoughts and fearful thoughts may come on, sometimes lasting for moments, sometimes going on endlessly with the dreadful awareness that they cannot be turned off.

Anxiety disorders have traditionally been treated by psychiatrists with addictive medications such a Xanax or Valium. More recently, antidepressants have been used. Little long-term success has been seen with either.

Schizophrenia

This is a disorder that at one time was described as being as high as one out of 100 in the general population. It is now down to 150 in 100,000, a much smaller number.

This is the most serious of mental illnesses. The American Psychiatric Association publication "Let's Talk about Mental Illness" states that the profession has developed treatments that allow *most* persons with schizophrenia to work, live with their families and enjoy friends. *This is simply not true.*

Schizophrenia is a disorder that starts in the late teens or early 20s, affects the way a person thinks, feels and acts—affects every aspect of their existence. Hallucinations, delusions, bizarre behavior and agitation are common and are the so-called positive symptoms. In front of their eyes, people see their loved ones deteriorate, almost in an Alzheimer fashion, from being normal to becoming a strange shell of their former selves.

What distinguishes schizophrenia from other disorders with psychiatric symptoms (and these are many) is the presence of the so-called "negative symptoms." The face loses the capacity to show feelings and emotions (affect). There is severe social withdrawal and an apathy so intense that people may be mute, talk gibberish, talk in a monotone or not be able to communicate their basic needs. They may not be able to dress, clothe or feed themselves. They may seem completely frozen with apathy as in catatonia.

The problem is that at one time almost anyone with hallucinations or paranoia would be diagnosed as schizophrenic. These patients would include those who are now more likely to be diagnosed as manic-depressive, multiple personality disorder, severe anxiety symptoms, borderline personality disorder, antisocial personality disorder, and people who suffer from unacceptable sexual habits and perversions.

Throughout the 1940s and 1950s they were either locked up, given shock therapy or even lobotomized. From the 1950s onward, because of the invention of the "magic" drug Thorazine, they have been treated with these medications which are often deadly and crippling and always uncomfortable. *The danger is that many treatable disorders have been previously labeled as schizophrenic.* The numbers have now dramatically decreased from one out of a hundred to a little over one out of a thousand through an increasing accuracy of diagnosis. State of the art diagnostic methods and research now show indications of brain abnormalities and schizophrenia through techniques such as PET (positron emission tomography) scanning, computerized electroencephalograms and MRI (magnetic resonance imaging) techniques. Genetic, autoimmune (abnormalities where the body fights itself) and viral disorders are now considered as possible factors in causing schizophrenia.

Other Illnesses

There are other illnesses that often make a person look psychotic. (In our society, psychotic is often equivalent to "crazy.") In fact, most people who are truly psychotic often don't recognize this. Psychosis in the way that the term is used here points to the presence of hallucinations and delusions and the less easily defined "thought disorder."

These include brain disorders such as Huntington's Chorea, Parkinson's disease, viral disorders of the brain such as:

Creutzfeldt-Jakob disease
AIDS-related encephalopathy
Nutrition-related encephalopathy
Alcohol-related encephalopathy
Diabetes-related encephalopathy
Reactions to medications
Temporal lobe epilepsy
Endocrine disorders of the thyroid and adrenals

These all can masquerade as mental illness. Brain tumors can often make the person look as if they are having psychiatric symptoms. A very thorough medical examination that involves neurologic, endocrine, immunologic and genetic workup, examination of various neurotransmitters and hormones in the body, plus appropriate psychologic and neuropsychologic testing may be helpful in differentiating and often treating these symptoms more completely.

1. "Let's Talk about Mental Illness," *American Psychiatric Press,* 1987.

NINETEEN

Medication:
A Double-Edged
Sword

To a lesser degree than with other medical illnesses, medications can be useful in serious psychiatric illnesses. The problem is that medications are almost always used wrongly or excessively in co-dependents and abuse survivors. Being a group that is often quick to look for outside "fixes," as well as being influenced by the authority of physicians who have little first-hand training and knowledge in problems related to ACoAs, addictions and co-dependency, the danger of misuse and the abuse of medications are multiplied.

Below is a list of medications that are currently prescribed by psychiatrists, internists and family practitioners. It is important to be armed with knowledge so you can make good decisions.

Antipsychotics. Also known as *major tranquilizers* or *neuroleptics.* These medications have been used since the 1950s for controlling the so-called psychotic symptoms which in the past have been synonymous with schizophrenia. Antipsychotics are used as a chemical straitjacket to "control" violent behavior, even though violent behavior itself may not be due to psychosis.

These drugs include Thorazine, Mellaril, Serentil, Navane, Stelazine, Trilafon, Loxitane, Moban, Prolixin, Haldol. Haldol is 100 times stronger than Thorazine by milligram comparison. The *immediate side effects* of these medications include sedation, especially for Thorazine, Mellaril and Serentil but also what are described as dys·tonic reactions (uncontrollable and unbalanced contractions of muscles, causing discomfort and pain). They can make you feel like your body is in a vise and you are being twisted. The tongue becomes thick and numb in the mouth so you cannot swallow your own saliva. A terrible restlessness (akathisia) takes over and you cannot sit still or be comfortable in any position, causing the pacing so commonly seen in psychiatric hospitals.

Here is a quote from someone who took it, firsthand. Jack Henry Abbott in *In the Belly of the Beast,*[1] states:

> *Prolixin is the worst I've experienced. One injection lasts for two weeks. Every two weeks you receive an injection. These drugs, in this family, do not calm or sedate the nerves. They attack. They attack from so deep within you, you cannot locate the source of pain. The drugs turn your nerves in upon yourself, against your will, your resistance, your resolve, are directed at your tissues, your own muscles, reflexes. These drugs are designed to render you so totally involved with yourself physically that all you can do is concentrate your entire being on holding yourself together (tying your shoes, for example). You cannot cease trembling. From all of these drugs you can get Parkinson's reaction, a physical reaction identical to Parkinson's disease. The muscles of your jawbone go berserk, so that you bite the insides of your mouth, your jaw locks, and the pain throbs. For hours every day this will occur. The spinal column stiffens so that you can hardly move your head or your neck and sometimes you bend backwards like a bow and you cannot stand up.*
>
> *The pain grinds into your fiber. Your vision is so blurred that you cannot read. You ache with restlessness, so you feel you have to walk, to pace. And then as soon as you start pacing, the opposite occurs to you—you must sit and rest. Back and forth, up and down you go in pain you cannot locate. In such wretched anxiety,*

you are overwhelmed, because you cannot get relief even when breathing. Sometimes a groan or a whimper rises inside you to the point it comes out involuntarily and people look at you curiously, so you suppress the noise as if it were a belch—the sound that is wrung out of your soul.

The person shuffles with short steps and with a stoop, without moving their arms and shoulders. These drugs can also affect the liver, the heart, the skin and the blood system, as well as the brain. It causes both impotence as well as painful retrograde ejaculation. It poisons the richest, most creative part of your brain (the cerebral cortex). It is what is described as GABA-toxic. GABA is the juice that fuels the most creative part of your brain.

And yet, these are the less dangerous and short-term effects. A more startling and serious effect is what is described as neuroleptic malignant syndrome. This severe reaction kills 4,000 people in this country every year who get major tranquilizers. It causes 30,000 people to become extremely ill to the point of having coma and confusion and needing to be hospitalized.

Anytime a person takes these medications for over three months, depending upon the dosage of the medications and the age of the person, they run the risk of developing what is described as *tardive dyskinesia.* Tardive dyskinesia is a disorder of the basal ganglia which is the "motor" of the brain and, in a sense, of the mind. Though painless, tardive dyskinesia makes a person have uncontrollable movements of their body—starting out with wormlike writhing of the tongue and going on to affect the muscles of the face which twist and grimace for no apparent reason. This progresses with continued use until the whole body twists uncontrollably in a snake-like manner.

What is even more serious, in my opinion, is the fact that these drugs affect the motivational apparatus of the brain. The percentage of people who suffer this permanent disorder which may be due to actual brain injury varies, according to reports from 15-25 percent, even though there are reports that in long-term users and older people it might be as high as 60 percent.

To take medications with life-threatening and permanent side effects for life-threatening illnesses such as end-stage heart disease, cancer or organ transplant is one thing. But these medications are being given to physically healthy people who come to their doctors complaining of depression, agitation, anxiety and hallucinations and wind up dead—4,000 every year.

Prolixin deconoate, a once-a-month or twice-weekly shot, is extensively used in prisons and community mental health centers for patients with "poor compliance." These have some of the worst side effects.

The Supreme Court has recently decided that psychiatrists can medicate prisoners against their will with these medications. I am personally aware of people in prisons who have died through the use of these medications.

Artane and Cogentin, medications that are given for side effects, can often make the person more psychotic. It has the same basic chemical actions as jimson weed (datura or loco weed).

Anti-anxiety medications. Also called minor tranquilizers. These include Librium, Valium, Serax, Ativan, Centrax, Xanax and Tranxene. These medications have limited usefulness and in my opinion are appropriate only for very brief periods of time for people who are dealing with a known and time-limited source of anxiety, for example, someone who is about to have a surgical procedure. Here again, reassurance, explanation and relaxation techniques have often been shown to be just as helpful.

Valium can be very helpful for acute back injury with muscle spasms but not for chronic back spasms or chronic pain. Effects on the central nervous system are mainly as a depressant, the same as alcohol. In small doses they make a person feel less inhibited, more relaxed, and take away the dry mouth, choking, pounding of the heart, hypervenilation and the tremors often seen in anxiety disorders. [This can also be accomplished with nonaddictive medications such as Propranolol (Inderal).] In large doses, just like alcohol, they make a person lose control and often become irrational, irritable and even psychotic. In large doses and in combination with alcohol, they can cause severe central nervous system depression to the point that a person may stop breathing. These are common drugs of overdosing and are universally prescribed for everything from sore feet, back and shoulders to menstrual cramps, migraine headaches and insomnia and as "mother's little helper" for women who complain to their family practitioners too much.

The most serious problem that these medications have is their extreme addictive potential and the dangers related to sudden withdrawal. Sudden withdrawal, especially after long periods of use (weeks and months) in large doses can cause seizures, high blood pressure and irregular heartbeat. I have had many patients develop seizures severe enough to dislocate shoulders, lose teeth and crack their heads. The seizures are described as the grand mal type.

The danger of addiction is greatest within the co-dependent/ addict community where there is often an endless "black hole" of overwhelming anxiety that, unlike someone who is going for surgery, has no name or face, cause, beginning or end. So once started, people get used to taking them. They feel better and then they are compelled to keep on increasing the dose endlessly. Cutting the dose down brings on overwhelming, unbearable, terrifying anxiety, panic, phobic and obsessional symptoms. In my opinion, they are just as dangerous as alcohol and because they are prescribed and "legal" (and don't show on your breath), they are more easily abused by women than alcohol itself.

Sedatives. These are also described as "downers" and act just like Valium but are less commonly prescribed these days. (They include Miltown, Equanil and Quaalude.) They can, however, be even more dangerous because of their severe central nervous system depression and their potential for cardiorespiratory failure. Psychiatric symptoms of use and abuse consist of confusion, depression, mood swings, psychosis and blackouts. This is true for Valium-like drugs and can happen even with "medical uses" like back pain when used for long periods of time (disinhibition).

Hypnotics. These medications are used to treat insomnia and other sleep problems which are universally present in addicts in second stage recovery, as well as in co-dependents. These include Halcion, Dalmane, Restoril, Chloral Hydrate and the more dangerous and often less prescribed medications such as Seconal, Nembutal and Doriden. Appropriate use of these drugs may be for a few days for someone who has severe pain problems. Use beyond three weeks usually causes worsening of the sleep problem. Abuse and addiction to these drugs are common, so they are very dangerous to people in recovery.

The side effects of these hypnotic medications include confusion, coordination problems, mood swings, depression, extreme daytime sleepiness and the risk of overdosing.

My advice to you is don't become involved with these drugs if you are in recovery. If you cannot sleep it means it is time to take inventory.

Lithium. Lithium is a mood stabilizer and is not addictive. The single appropriate use is for "bringing down" people who are manic and decreasing mood swings where it can be used prophylactically. However, in my experience, there is too much arbitrary diagnosis of ıic-depressive illness based on mood swings. People coming from dysfunctional family backgrounds, co-dependents and addicts in second-stage recovery almost always show proneness towards mood swings and may be put on these medications without adequate investigation of their real problem.

These medications are very toxic and have a small "therapeutic window." Small doses don't help and larger doses cause the person to have violent side effects which include confusion, loss of consciousness, convulsions, ataxia (loss of balance and incoordination), tremors, nausea, vomiting and diarrhea. Lithium is toxic to the heart, thyroid gland and the kidneys, and there is some suggestion recently that it might be toxic to the brain. It also causes weight gain. Even with appropriate use it can cause damage to the kidneys. Blood and urine tests to check for deteriorating kidney function are essential. Thyroid tests, electrocardiogram and kidney function tests are essential before these medications are started and should be done periodically throughout the time that they are used. Lithium has also been used in an attempt to treat a wide variety of disorders, especially those that have a cyclical nature, and these include periodic headaches, premenstrual syndrome, episodic violent behavior and recurrent depression.

Antidepressants. Antidepressants are a class of medications that have been used to treat depression just like aspirin is used to treat fever. And just like aspirin will not treat the infection or the pus pocket or abscess that causes a fever, antidepressants will not treat the cause of these depressions—or cure it.

Antidepressants are not addictive.[2]

Some important things that you need to know about antidepressants, since they are so commonly used, and since insurance companies put tremendous amounts of pressure on psychiatrists to use them, are as follows:

They don't make a person feel better as soon as they start taking them, in the sense that Valium will make a person immediately less anxious about a half hour after they take it. It may take anywhere from ten days to three weeks before they show any response to the medication.

Antidepressants have serious and often life-threatening complications and side effects. The most serious side effects are seizures, heart blocks (especially dangerous for people who have heart problems), irregularities of the heart and sudden drop in blood pressure on sitting up or standing up with a possible loss of consciousness. Skull and hip fractures from falls and sudden deaths have been noted, especially among the older population. Rarely, the body's capacity to effectively fight infections may be affected by these drugs.

Less serious but disturbing side effects which are commonly seen include dizziness, headaches, blurred vision, hallucinations, nightmares, ringing in the ears, dry mouth, chest palpitations, tremors, constipation, difficulty urinating, fatigue, impaired concentration and loss of sex drive. *Very depressing* side effects.

One of the antidepressants, Desyrel, however, has been known to cause the opposite in terms of what it does to a person sexually. It causes priapism—a condition where the person gets an uncontrollable erection and cannot bring it down. This is a painful condition which may need surgical intervention in extreme cases.

Antidepressants have to be taken in adequate quantities. Seventy-five percent of the people who take antidepressants don't take enough of it to make it work. It has to be started in small quantities and gradually increased in dose as tolerated. This may take weeks.

Laboratory tests, including studies of the blood, electrocardiogram and electroencephalogram (brain wave tests) should be done prior to taking these medications and may need to be repeated.

All antidepressants may not work for all depressed patients and many may not respond to any antidepressant. They may also stop working after a time.

They have to be taken daily for many months or even years.

Thousands of people overdose on antidepressants since they are primarily prescribed for patients who are depressed and often suicidal. They are sometimes prescribed for migraine, obsessive-compulsive disorder, panic disorder, enuresis and insomnia, as well as for chronic pain.

As the antidepressant medication begins to work, the sluggish, suicidal person may often find the energy to act on their suicidal thoughts and actually go on to attempt it. It is often best that with the combination of side effects and the risk of suicide that these medications be used in an inpatient setting or with extremely close monitoring by a medical doctor if they are to be used in an outpatient setting.

Antidepressants are mainly of two classes: tricyclics and MAO (monoamino oxidase) inhibitors. Tricyclics include medications such as Amitriptyline (Elavil), Nortriptyline (Pamelor), Imipramine (Tofranil), Desipramine (Norpramin). MAO inhibitors include medications such as Parnate, Nardil and Marplan. MAO inhibitors can cause life-threatening-hypertensive crisis with the risk of stroke if a very strict diet is not adhered to (Tyramine-free diet—ask your doctor to give you the diet in writing). Newer antidepressants such as Desyrel and Prozac have lesser side effects.

Nevertheless, to be fair, antidepressants may have a role in treating some kinds of depression as long as the reasons for causing the depression are being *actively addressed,* concurrently and consistently. Addicts and co-dependents are always in danger of looking towards outside fixes and neglecting internal resources and this danger is there with antidepressants as well. Make sure that all the other work of recovery has been done or is being done. And like a crutch or a cast around a broken leg, get rid of it once your leg has healed and strengthened.

Other medications used for treating psychiatric problems.

1. *Tegretol* is used as a mood stabilizer instead of, or in addition to, Lithium and also in attempts to decrease rage and violent behavior. It is routinely used to treat seizures, including temporal lobe epilepsy which often mimics emotional mental disorders. It has also been prescribed routinely to treat trigeminal neuralgia. It is experimentally used to treat sexual perversions and may be less harmful than chemical castration.

   In my opinion, all sexual acting out, molestation and perverse behavior come from sexual abuse in childhood and the roots have to be addressed in treatment, not the fruits.

   Tegretol can cause cardiac irregularities, heart blocks, liver problems and seizures. A rare but extremely important side effect is a fatal loss of white blood cells (agranulocytosis)— loss of the stippled white blood cells that help the body fight acute (but not chronic) infections.

2. *Anafranil* is the new "drug of choice" for obsessive-compulsive behavior. Once again, obsessive-compulsive behavior is a symptom of any underlying fear, insecurity and unhappiness that medications cannot fix. Anafranil can cause life-threatening blood disorders.

3. *Clozaril* is the new drug for schizophrenia. While it is not known to cause the previously-described side effects such as tardive dyskinesia, it can cause serious and sometimes fatal blood disorders.

4. *Propranolol* (Inderal) is a "beta blocker" used to decrease hypertension but it can also decrease the bodily symptoms of anxiety such as palpitations, tremulousness, pounding in the chest and dry mouth. It has also been used to control violent behavior.

5. **Clonidine** is an "alpha agonist" used to treat hypertension. It has been used to detoxify people from heroin. It also causes a decrease in anxiety. It can cause cramps, sweating and low blood pressure to the point of fainting.

6. **Isoptin** (Verapamil) is a "calcium channel blocker" used as an antihypertensive medication routinely; it has more recently been used as a mood stabilizer.

7. **L-tryptophan,** currently unavailable, is an amino acid that was used to help people sleep. It has been taken off the market secondary to a suspicion that it sometimes causes fatal eosinophilia.

None of the above medications are known to be addictive. But let me emphasize by repetition: don't use crutches. Look inside yourself. Take inventory. You have the power within. *Everything is possible with love, truth, courage and hard work.*

---

1. Abbott, Jack Henry, **In the Belly of the Beast,** New York: Random House, 1981.

2. Some antidepressants such as Elavil (Amitriptyline) have sometimes been used for getting a high by teenagers. It is the Atropinelike effect which gives the "buzz." The high involves feeling hot and flushed with pounding heart, blurred vision and often hallucinations.

TWENTY

From Enslavement
To Empowerment

Enslavement—to drugs, alcohol, sexual addictions, fears, phobias, panic and anxiety, rage and work, and most of all, to relationships—is not what we were born with. This is the baggage, the armor, the cloud that we have taken on—taken on without any control at a time when we truly had no choices and continued unconsciously because of not knowing better.

Getting rid of the toxic baggage, of the bad dreams of your childhood, growing up in a dysfunctional family environment, coming out of the cloud of addictions, allows you increasingly to feel and taste freedom. Freedom to make choices, freedom to play, freedom to be creative and freedom to be with others and enjoy others without the threat of losing yourself.

It is, as I have said many times before, not an easy journey. There is a kind of comfort in enslavement and a kind of fear in newfound freedom. People used to being enslaved may fear to make the change. Some will feel that it is better to *belong,* even if it means that they belong by a chain around the neck. Sometimes the chain is real (as I have descirbed with some of my patients) and at other times the chain is a high-priced diamond necklace, material wealth, addictive drugs, "a position" at work, a relationship that is destructive.

You have to decide about making the change from enslavement to empowerment.

From Pathologic Enmeshment To Joyous Connectedness

From love that binds to love that frees, this is the journey for all of us, abused or otherwise. It takes us from being chained or fighting being chained to people in our lives to where we will feel glorious and strengthened by the love that we feel towards and from others in our lives.

It comes about as you follow the steps of recovery, by becoming in touch with yourself, your strengths, your weaknesses; by accepting and admitting powerlessness over the weaknesses and the defects of others in our lives—parents, spouse, friends, employers—and by respecting the strength and recognizing the love of others in your life. It includes being honest without blaming and taking honest criticism without feeling put down or feeling unloved.

Yes, it is true that some of us have murderers and rapists for parents. But most of us don't. Most people, especially people coming from a background of abuse, want more than anything else not to repeat the mistakes and the shortcomings of their parents. But because of the armor that they have built to protect themselves in their own growing up, they lose touch with their true feelings and build walls within to hide their feelings from themselves and walls without to hide their feelings from others.

And with these walls, these unhealthy defenses, they play out their hurts, hurting themselves and others in the process and taking away from the glory and joy of being a child of God.

Recovery is not something that you will wake up to one fine morning. Recovery is not unloading at an AA meeting and feeling that everything is "okay."

By definition, recovery is a process.

I think about recovery as climbing a mountain. Initially it is steep and slippery and you may fall many times, hurt and have blood under your nails from having to hold on hour after hour, day after day, week after week, month after month, year after year. But if you work the program with consistency, honesty and courage, always keeping your mind on your spiritual self, you will find that the terrain becomes easier. And one day you will look around and find that, indeed, life is beginning to make sense—that truly change has taken place and there is magic in your life.

REFERENCES/BIBLIOGRAPHY

Psychiatric Medical Abuses

1. **The Age Of Madness.** A history of involuntary hospitalization. Thomas H. Szasz, M.D., Anchor Press Doubleday, 1959.

2. **The Right To Be Different.** Deviancy and enforced therapy. Nicholas M. Kittrie, Johns Hopkins Press, 1971.

3. **The Manufacture Of Madness.** A comparative study of the inquisition and the mental health movement. Thomas H. Szasz, M.D., Harper Colophon, New York, 1970.

4. **Sexual Exploitation In Professional Relationships.** Edited by Grant O. Gabbard, M.D., American Psychiatric Press, Washington, D.C., 1989.

5. **Sex In The Therapy Hour.** A case of professional incest. Carolyn M. Bates and Emmett M. Brodsky, Guilford Press, New York, 1989.

6. **Sexual Exploitation Of Patients By Health Professionals.** N.W. Burgess and Carol R. Hartman, editors, Praeger, New York, 1986.

7. **Sexual Intimacy Between Therapists And Patients.** Kenneth S. Pope and Jacqueline Bouhoutsos, Praeger, New York, 1986.

8. **Sex In The Forbidden Zone.** Peter Rutter, M.D., Jeremy P. Tucher, Incorporated, Los Angeles, 1989.

9. **The Assault On Truth.** Freud's suppression of the seduction theory. Jeffrey Masson, Farrar, Straus and Giroux, New York, 1984.

10. **Great And Desperate Cures.** The rise and decline of psycho-surgery and other radical treatments of mental illness. Elliott Valenstein, Basic Books, New York, 1986.

11. **Will There Really Be A Morning?** Frances Farmer, Little, Brown and Company, 1972.

12. **In The Belly Of The Beast.** Letters from prison. Jack Henry Abbott, Random House, New York, 1981.

Infancy, Childhood And Parenting

1. **Childhood In Contemporary Cultures.** Edited by Margaret Mead and Martha Wolsenstein, University of Chicago Press, 1955.

2. **The Scope Of Child Analysis.** Victor Smirnoff, International Universities Press, 1971.

3. **Insights From The Blind.** Comparative studies of blind and sighted children. Selma Fraiberg, Basic Books, 1977.

4. **Childhood And Society.** Eric H. Ericson, W. Norton and Company, Inc., New York, 1950.

5. **First Feelings.** Milestones in the emotional development of your baby and child. From birth to age 4. Stanley Greenspan, M.D. and Nancy Thorndike Greenspan, Viking Press, 1985.

6. **Parent Infant Relationship.** Paul M. Taylor, M.D., Grune and Stratton, New York, 1980.

7. **Hallucinations In Children.** Daniel Crolsky, M.D. and William Chambers, M.D., American Psychiatric Press, Washington, D.C., 1986.

8. **Clinical Studies In Childhood Psychosis.** Twenty-five years in collaborative treatment and research at the Langley Porter Children's Service. S.A. Szurek, M.D. and I. N. Berlin, M.D., Brunner/Mazel, New York, 1973.

9. **Suicide Among Youth.** Perspectives on risk and prevention. Cynthia R. Pfiffer, American Psychiatric Press, Washington, D.C., 1989.

10. **Interpersonal World Of Infant.** A view from psychoanalysis and developmental psychology. Daniel N. Stern, Basic Books, Inc., New York, 1985.

11. **The First Year Of Life.** Rene A. Spitz, International Universities Press, New York, 1965.

12. **The Early Development Of Affect And Mood.** Bulletin of the Menninger Clinic, Volume 43, No. 1, January, 1979.

13. **Deprivation of Maternal Care.** A reassessment of its effects. Mary B. Insworth, R. G. Andrey, Robert G. Harlow, S. Lebovici, Margaret Mead, Dame G. Truth, Barbara Wootton; World Health Organization, Geneva, 1962.

14. **Clinical Infant Intervention Research Program.** Selected overview and discussion. National Institute of Mental Health, Department of Health, Education and Welfare, DHEW Publications (ADMW8-748), 1979.

15. **The First Twelve Months Of Life — Your Baby's Growth Month By Month.** General editor Frank Copeland, Bantam Books, New York, 1983.

16. **Developmental Psychiatry.** Michael Rutter, American Psychiatric Press, Washington, D.C., 1980.

17. **Studies Of Children.** Monographs in Psychosocial Development, Felton Earl. Academic Publications, New York, 1980.

18. **Attachment.** John Bowlby, Basic Books, New York, 1969.

19. **The Developmental Approach To Childhood Psychopathology.** Humberto Nagera, M.D., New York, Jason Aronson, 1981.

20. **Separation, Attachment And Loss,** Volume II. Anxiety and Anger. John Bowlby, The Tavistock Institute of Human Relationships, Basic Books, 1973.

21. **Through Pediatrics To Psychoanalysis.** D. W. Winnicott, Basic Books, New York, 1975.

22. **The Maturational Processes And The Facilitating Environment.** Studies in the theory of emotional development. D. W. Winnicott, London International Universities Press, 1965.

23. **Developmental Neuropsychobiology.** William T. Greunoth and Janice M. Juraska, Academic Press, Inc., Orlando, Florida, 1986.

24. **Physiological And Behavioral Processes In Early Maternal Deprivation.** M. A. Harper, from **Physiology, Emotion And Psychosomatic Illness.** A Ciba Foundation Symposium, Ciba Foundation, 1972.

25. **Loss — Sadness And Depression.** John Bowlby, Basic Books, 1980.

26. **Baboon Mothers And Infants.** Jane Altmann, Harvard University Press, Cambridge, Massachusetts, 1980.

27. **The Chimpanzees Of Gombi.** Patterns of behavior. Jane Goodall, Harvard University Press, Cambridge, Massachusetts, 1986.

28. **Relationship Disturbances In Early Childhood, A Developmental Approach.** Arnold A. Sommeroff and Robert N. Emde, Basic Books, New York, 1989.

29. **Prisoners Of Childhood.** The drama of the gifted child and the search for the true self. Alice Miller, Basic Books, 1981.

30. **The Infant Mind.** Richard Restak, M.D., Doubleday and Company, New York, 1986.

31. **In The Shadow Of Man.** Jane Goodall, Houghton Mifflin Company, 1971.

Child Abuse

1. **The Silent Children.** A parent's guide to prevention of child sexual abuse, Linda Tschirhart Sanford.

2. **Child Abuse.** The developing child series, Ruth S. Kempe and C. Henry Kempe. Harvard University Press, Cambridge, Massachusetts, 1978.

3. **For Your Own Good.** Hidden cruelty in child-rearing and the roots of violence. Alice Miller, Farrar, Straus, Giroux, New York, 1984.

4. **Thou Shalt Not Be Aware.** Society's betrayal of the child. Alice Miller, New American Library, 1986.

Mind/Body Medicine

1. "Nervous System Disease and Systemic Lupus Erythematoses." Harry G. Bluestein, *Immunology and Allergy clinics of North America,* August, 1988.

2. **Neuroimmune Disorders.** W. B. Saunders Company, 1988.

3. **Bereavement, Depression, Stress And Immunity.** Marvin Stein, Neuromodulation of Immunity, R. Guilleman, Raven Press, New York, 1985.

4. **Stress In Human Immunologic Competency.** Neuromodulation of immunity. R. Guilleman, Raven Press, New York, 1985.

5. **Psychoneuroendocrinology.** Topics in Neuroendocrinology. Joseph B. Martin and Seymour Reichlin. Contemporary Neurology Series, F. A. Davis Co., 1987.

6. **Explorations In Psychoneuroimmunology.** Ruth Lloyd, Grune and Stratton.

7. **Minding The Body, Mending The Mind.** Joan Borysenko, Ph.D., Addison Wellsley Company, Reading, Massachusetts, 1987.

8. **The Relaxation Response.** Herbert Benson, M.D., William Morrow and Company, Inc., New York, 1975.

9. **Beyond The Relaxation Response.** Herbert Benson, M.D. with William Proctor, Times Books, 1984, New York.

10. **Psychosomatic Illness Review.** Wilford Dorfman, M.D., Academy of Psychosomatic Medicine, McMillan Publishing Co., New York, 1985.

11. **Psychosomatic Concepts.** Roy R. Grinker, M.D., Jason Aronson, New York, 1973.

12. **Phenomenology In Treatment Of Psychophysiological Disorders.** Marianne Sand, Ismet Karansan, Alex B. Khaalmy, Robert Y. Williams, Este Books Publications, Inc., New York, 1982.

13. **Chronobiology In Psychiatric Disorders.** Angelos Halaris, Elsevier Science Publishing Co., Inc., New York, 1987.

14. **Mind As Healer, Mind As Slayer: A Holistic Approach To Preventing Stress Disorders.** Bell Publishing Company, New York, 1977.

Post-Traumatic Stress Disorder/Dissociative Disorders

1. **Post-traumatic Stress Disorder In Children.** Spencer Eth, M.D. and Robert Pynoos, M.D., M.C.H., American Psychiatric Press, Washington, D.C., 1984.

2. **Unity And Multiplicity.** Multilevel consciousness of self in hypnosis, psychiatric disorders and mental health. John Beahrs, M.D., Brunner/Mazel, New York, 1982.

3. **Multiple Personality, Allied Disorders And Hypnosis.** Eugene L. Bliss, Oxford University Press, New York, 1986.

4. **Repetition And Trauma.** Towards a Telemonmic Theory of Psychoanalysis. Max M. Stern. The Analytic Press, Postville, New Jersey, 1988.

5. **The Trauma Of War.** Treatment and Recovery in Vietnam Veterans. Steven M. Sonenberg, M.D., Arthur S. Flank, Jr., M.D., John A. Talbot, National Psychiatric Press, Washington, D.C., 1985.

6. **Post-Traumatic Stress Disorder: Diagnosis, Treatment And Legal Issues.** C. B. Scrignar, M.D., Prager, New York, 1984.

7. **Psychologic Trauma.** Bessel Van Der Kolk, M.D., American Psychiatric Press, 1987.

8. **Childhood Antecedents Of Multiple Personality.** Richard Kluft, M.D., Ph.D., American Psychiatric Press, Washington, D.C., 1985.

9. **The Dark Side Of Families.** Current Family Violence Research. David Finkelhor, Richard J. Gelles, Gerald T. Hotling, Murray A. Straus, Sage Publications, Beverly Hills, CA, 1983.

10. **Treatment Of Multiple Personality Disorder.** Bennett J. Braun, American Psychiatric Press, Washington, D.C., 1986.

11. **Multiple Personality Disorder.** Diagnosis, Clinical Features and Treatment. Colin A. Ross, M.D., John Wiley and Sons, 1989.

12. **Bodies Under Seige.** Self-Mutilation in Culture and Psychiatry. Armando R. Favazza, M.D., Johns Hopkins University Press, Baltimore, Maryland, 1987.

13. **On Some Roots Of Creativity.** Henry Crystal, M.D., Psychiatric Clinics of North America (Hemispheric Specialization), W. B. Saunders, September, 1988.

14. **Diagnosis And Treatment Of Multiple Personality Disorder.** Frank Putnam, M.D., Guilford Press, New York, 1989.

15. **Psychoanalysis,** the Kohut Seminars in Self-Psychology and Psychotherapy with Adolescents and Young Adults. Miriam Elson, W. Norton Company, New York, 1987.

16. **Treating The Self.** Elements of Clinical Self-Psychology. Ernest S. Wolf, Guilford Press, New York, 1988.
17. **Internal World And External Reality.** Object Relations Theory Applied. Otto F. Kernberg, M.D., New York, Jason Aronson, 1980.
18. **Splitting And Projective Identification.** James S. Grotstein, Jason Aronson, New York, 1981.
19. **Advances In Self-Psychology.** Arnold Goldberg, M.D., International Universities Press, 1980.
20. **Do I Dare Disturb The Universe?** A Memorial to Wilfred R. Bion. James S. Grotstein, Causera Press, Beverly Hills, CA, 1981.
21. **The Borderline Syndromes.** Constitution, Personality and Adaptation. Michael H. Stone, McGraw Hill, New York, 1980.
22. **How Does Analysis Cure?** Heinz Kohut. University of Chicago Press, 1984.
23. **Father-Daughter Incest.** Judith Lewis Herman. Harvard University Press, Cambridge, Mass., 1981.

Body Work

1. **Healing Massage Techniques.** Holistic, Classic and Emerging Methods. Frances Tappan, Ed.D., M.A., Appleton and Lange, Norwalk, Connecticut, 1988.
2. **The Image And Appearance Of The Human Body.** Paul Schilder, M.D., International Universities Press, New York, 1950.
3. **The Skin Ego — A Psychoanalytic Approach To Self.** Didier Anzien, Yale University Press, 1989.
4. **The Mind Of The Skin.** Anthropology and Human Nature. Ashley Montagu, Porter Sargent, Boston, 1957.
5. **Stimulation And The Preterm Infant.** The Limits of Plasticity. Clinics and Perinatology, Barry Lester, Ph.D., and Edward Tronick, Ph.D., March, W. B. Saunders, 1990.
6. **The Body As A Medium Of Expression.** E. P. Dutton, 1975. *The Comparative Study Of Nonverbal Communication.* R. A. Hinde.

Psychiatry/Psychology

1. **Treatment Of Psychiatric Disorders.** A task force report of the American Psychiatric Association. Washington, D.C., 1989.
2. **"The Psychiatric Patient's Right to Effective Treatment."** Implications of Osheroff vs. Chestnut Lodge by Gerald Klerman. *American Journal of Psychiatry,* Volume 147, No. 4, April, 1990.
3. **Law, Science And Psychiatric Malpractice.** A Response to Kerman's Indictment of Psychoanalytic Psychiatry by Alan Stone.
4. **Psychobiology Of Bulimia.** James Hudson, M.D. and Harrison G. Pope, Jr., M.D., Progress in Psychiatry, American Psychiatric Press, 1987.
5. **Personality Disorders: Diagnosis And Management.** John R. Lion, M.D., Williams and Wilkins Co., Baltimore, 1974.
6. **The Psychopath — A Comprehensive Study Of Antisocial Disorders And Behaviors.** William H. Reid, M.D., Brunner/Mazel, New York, 1978.

7. **A Comprehensive Approach To The Treatment Of Normal Weight Bulimia.** Walter H. Kaye, M.D., Harry E. Grwirtsman, M.D., Clinical Insights, American Psychiatric Press, Washington, D.C., 1985.

8. *The Bulletin Of The Menninger Clinic.* Volume 41, No. 5., September, 1977. Special Issue on Anorexia Nervosa.

9. **Functional Disorders Of Memory.** The Experimental Psychology Series. John S. Kihlstrom and Frederick J. Evans. Lawrence Elbron Associates, 1979, Postville, New Jersey.

10. **The Anatomy Of Hallucinations.** Fred H. Johnson, Nelson Paul, Chicago, 1978.

11. **Eating, Sleeping And Sexuality.** Treatment of Disorders in Basic Life Functions. Michael R. Zales, M.D., Brunner/Mazel, New York, 1982.

12. **The Diagnostic And Statistical Manual Of Mental Disorders, fourth edition.** American Psychiatric Association, 1989.

13. **Sleep And Its Disorders.** J. D. Parkes, W. B. Saunders, England, 1985.

14. **The Comprehensive Textbook Of Psychiatry, fifth edition.** Harold I. Kaplan, M.D. and Benjamin S. Sadok, M.D., Williams and Wilkins Co., Baltimore, MD, 1989.

15. **The Borderline: Current Empirical Research.** Thomas H. McGlasham, M.D., Progress in Psychiatry Series, American Psychiatric Press, 1985.

Medications

1. **Psychiatric Pharmacosciences Of Children And Adolescents.** Charles Popper, M.D., American Psychiatric Press, Washington, D.C., 1984.

2 **Lithium Encyclopedia For Clinical Practice.** James W. Jefferson, M.D., John H. Greist, M.D., Debra L. Ackerman, M.S., Judith Carol, B.A., American Psychiatric Press, 1987.

3 **The Use Of Anticonvulsants In Psychiatry.** Recent Advances. Susan L. McElroy, M.D., and Harrison G. Pope, M.D., Oxford Healthcare, Inc., Clifton, New Jersey, 1988.

4. **The Neuroleptic Malignant Syndrome And Related Conditions.** Arthur Lazurus, M.D., Steven Mann, M.D., Stanley M. Caroff, M.D., American Psychiatric Press, Washington, D.C., 1989.

5. **Drugs And The Brain.** Solomon H. Snyder. Scientific American Library, New York, 1986.

6. **Tardive Dyskinesia And Neuroleptics.** From Dogma to Reason. Daniel E. Casey, M.D., and George Gardos, M.D., American Psychiatric Press, Inc., Washington, D.C., 1986.

7. **The Psychopharmacology Of The Limbic System.** Michael R. Trimble, Oxford University Press, 1985.

General

1. Alcoholics Anonymous ("The Big Book").

2. **Juvenile Homicide.** Elissa B. Benedick, M.D. and Dewey G. Cornell, Ph.D., American Psychiatric Press, Washington, D.C., 1988.

3. **Aspects Of Epilepsy In Psychiatry.** Michael Trimble and Tom Browig, John Wiley and Sons, Ltd., 1986.

4. **Soft Neurologic Signs.** David B. Tupper, Ph.D., Grune and Stratton, Inc., Orlando, Florida, 1987.

5. **Cerebral Lateralization.** Biological Mechanisms, Associations and Pathologies. Normal Geschwind, M.D. and Albert M. Galaburda, M.D., Massachusetts Institute of Technology, 1987.

6. **Hormonal Modulation Of Memory.** Memory and the Brain. Larry Squires, Oxford University Press, 1987.

7. **The Language Of The Heart.** Bill W.'s Grapevine Writing, AA Grapevine Inc., New York, 1988.

8. **The Limbic System.** Functional Organization and Clinical Disorders. Benjamin K. Doane, M.D., Ph.D. and Kenneth Livingston, M.D., Raven Press, New York, 1986.

9. **Brain Imaging.** Applications in Psychiatry. Nancy C. Andresen, M.D., Ph.D., American Psychiatric Press, Washington, D.C., 1989.

10. **Principles Of Behavioral Neurology.** M. MarEl Masulam, M.D., F.A. Davis Co., Philadelphia, 1985.

11. **Psychiatry And Biology Of The Human Brain.** Steven Matthysse, Elsevier/North Holland, 1981.

12. **The Far Reaches Of Human Nature.** Abraham H. Maslow. Penguin Books, 1971.

13. **In Cold Blood.** Truman Capote. A true account of multiple murders and its consequences. New American Library, 1965.

14. **Man's Search For Meaning.** An Introduction to Logotherapy. Victor E. Frankel, Massachusetts, 1959.

15. **The Broken Brain.** The Biological Revolution in Psychiatry. Nancy C. Andreason, M.D., Ph.D., Harper and Row, New York, 1984.

16. **The Expressions Of Emotions In Men And Animals.** Charles Darwin, University of Chicago Press, 1965.

17. **Killer: A Journal Of Murder.** Thomas B. Gaddis and James O. Long, Fawcett Career Books, Greenwich, Connecticut, 1970.

18. **Out Of Bondage.** Linda Lovelace, Berkely Books, New York, 1986.

19. **The Natural History Of Alcoholism.** Causes, Patterns and Paths to Recovery. George E. Vaillant, Harvard University Press, Cambridge, Mass., 1983.